P9-CAP-300

Complete EnglishSmart

Revised and Updated!

Grade **3**

Grammar

Comprehension

Vocabulary

Writing

Usage

ISBN: 978-1-897457-03-0

Complete EnglishSmart Contents

ISBN: 978-1-897457-03-0

ISBN: 978-1-897457-03-0

ISBN: 978-1-897457-03-0

ISBN: 978-1-897457-03-0

NUNAVUT,
Canada's Newest Territory

Originally, Canada was made up of ten provinces and two northern territories called the Yukon and the Northwest Territories. On April 1, 1999, the Northwest Territories was divided into two parts. The new area to the east was called Nunavut.

Nunavut has the largest land area in Canada. It is almost 2,000,000 sq. km in area and makes up 1/5 of Canada. Its capital, Iqaluit, has a population of 4,000. Some villages in Nunavut have as few as 18 residents.

Because much of Nunavut is above the Arctic Circle, winter lasts about 9 months and is extremely cold. Most of Nunavut's soil is called "permafrost", which means that it stays frozen all year round. In spring and summer, there is daylight 24 hours a day.

Most people in Nunavut are Inuit. In the Inuktitut language, Inuit means "people". People use snowmobiles and planes to travel around in Nunavut. In the old days, the Inuit used dogsleds as the main form of transportation.

The seal was the most important animal to the Inuit. They made boots from sealskin and used the blubber for both lamp oil and food. A favourite food was "muktuk" – the blubber from whales. Today, half the population still hunt and fish for their food.

ISBN: 978-1-897457-03-0

Finding Information

A. Give short answers to the following questions.

1. What are the names of Canada's original territories before Nunavut?

    _____

2. Name the capital of Nunavut.

    _____

3. Why are Nunavut's winters so cold?

    _____

4. How long does winter last in Nunavut?

    _____

5. Why is Nunavut's soil called "permafrost"?

    _____

6. What are the two methods of transportation used in Nunavut?

    _____

7. What language do the Inuit people of Nunavut speak?

    _____

8. How did the Inuit people travel in the old days?

    _____

9. Which Arctic animal was the most important to the Inuit?

    _____

10. What is "muktuk"?

    _____

ISBN: 978-1-897457-03-0

Nouns

- A **Common Noun** is the general term for a person, place, thing, or an idea.

  Examples: person – boy, girl, man, woman

  place – house, school, store, building, farm

  thing – car, book, plant, bicycle, doll, computer

  idea – friendship, happiness, truth, feelings, thoughts

- A **Proper Noun** is the actual name of a specific person, place, or thing.

  Examples: person – John A. Macdonald, Wayne Gretzky, Britney Spears

  place – Toronto, Rogers Centre, Royal Ontario Museum, St. Joseph's School, Lake Ontario, Rocky Mountains

  thing – Chrysler, Barbie Doll, Kleenex

B. Put the nouns into the correct columns.

manager   farm   Mt. Albert   stickers   Mrs. Jones

CN Tower   joy   Moon River   school

Dr. Smith   truck   Avril Lavigne

Common Nouns	Proper Nouns

ISBN: 978-1-897457-03-0

Consonants

- A **Consonant** is any letter that is not a vowel (a,e,i,o,u).

C. **Add consonants to the vowels below. Try to form three words for each vowel.**

1. _____ u _____
   _____ u _____
   _____ u _____

2. _____ i _____
   _____ i _____
   _____ i _____

3. _____ o _____
   _____ o _____
   _____ o _____

4. _____ oo _____
   _____ oo _____
   _____ oo _____

5. _____ e _____
   _____ e _____
   _____ e _____

6. _____ ea _____
   _____ ea _____
   _____ ea _____

Missing Consonants

D. **Solve the consonant riddles. Place the consonant letters in the spaces provided.**

1. I'm a consonant that has a buzz when I fly.   _____

2. I can do this with my eyes wide open.   _____

3. I drink this in the morning instead of coffee.   _____

4. I like this kind of soup.   _____

5. You see with two of me.   _____

6. I'm the plural of the verb "is".   _____

7. Sometimes I mark the spot.   _____

8. I'm a blue bird and a baseball player.   _____

ISBN: 978-1-897457-03-0

What Makes up Our Universe?

Astronomers are scientists who study the universe. Some astronomers believe that at one time, all the stars and planets were joined together in one big lump. They think that the universe began as a result of a big explosion that happened about 15 billion years ago. They call this event the Big Bang.

It is thought that this explosion sent pieces of the universe flying off in various directions. As time passed, some of these pieces drifted together and formed galaxies. These galaxies continue to travel in space, making the universe bigger and bigger as time passes.

Astronomers have different ideas about the future of the universe. Some believe that it will continue to grow. Others think that the galaxies will drift back towards each other, reversing the Big Bang.

We live in a galaxy called the Milky Way. When you look at the sky on a clear night, you can see the stars and planets that make up the Milky Way. The Milky Way got its name because it looks like a white stream of light. There are about 1,000 billion stars in the Milky Way but we cannot see most of them.

It is believed that there are 100 billion galaxies in the universe. It is impossible to know how many billions of stars make up the entire universe. But, astronomers think that there are about 100 million trillion!

ISBN: 978-1-897457-03-0

Matching Facts

A. Match the information in Column A with the explanations in Column B.

Column A

1. Milky Way _____
2. galaxy _____
3. astronomers _____
4. 1,000 billion _____
5. Big Bang _____
6. 100 billion _____

Column B

A. happened 15 billion years ago

B. the galaxy that we live in

C. number of stars in the Milky Way

D. scientists who study the universe

E. number of galaxies in the universe

F. a collection of stars and planets

Further Thoughts

B. Answer the following questions.

1. Can you explain the Big Bang theory in your own words?

_____

_____

_____

_____

2. How did the Milky Way get its name?

_____

_____

_____

_____

ISBN: 978-1-897457-03-0

 **Verbs**

- A **Verb** is an action word in a sentence. It shows what the subject of the sentence is doing.

  Example: The boy ran home. "Ran" is the verb in this sentence.

C. Underline the verb in each sentence below.

1. The player dropped his stick.

2. The player shot the puck at the net.

3. The goalie fell to the ice.

4. The goalie missed the puck.

5. The coach encouraged the team.

6. The player raised his arms in celebration.

7. The crowd cheered wildly.

D. Choose a verb that would make sense for each sentence below. Try not to use the same verb twice.

dribbled	helped	called	swung	played
danced	bounced	chased	gathered	moved

1. The students _____ in the schoolyard.

2. They _____ on the monkey bars.

3. Some boys _____ basketball.

4. Some of the girls _____ the younger students.

5. A few children _____ balls.

6. The teacher _____ everyone to return to class.

ISBN: 978-1-897457-03-0

Vowels

- The **Vowels** – *a, e, i, o, u* – can have long or short vowel sounds.

  Examples: cat – has a short vowel sound

  plate – has a long vowel sound

  Note: the long vowel sound says the name of the actual letter.

E. Underline the vowel in each word and write "short" or "long" in the space provided.

1. plate _____

2. duck _____

3. pie _____

4. may _____

5. stick _____

6. toe _____

7. pop _____

8. clue _____

9. throw _____

F. Eavesdropping ... Can you figure out what the children are saying? Just fill in the vowels.

1. It is a b___a___tif___l d___y today.

2. Y___s, it ___s. Sh___ll we go o___ts___de?

3. L___t's go to th___ p___rk.

4. Wo___ld you l___ke to c___me t___ ___?

5. Th___nk yo___ f___r ask___ng m___ to jo___n you.

6. I'd l___ve to g___ to th___ p___rk. Sh___ll I br___ng

   a s___cc___r b___ll?

7. Lo___k. There's J___hn. L___t's ask h___m to come

   al___ng.

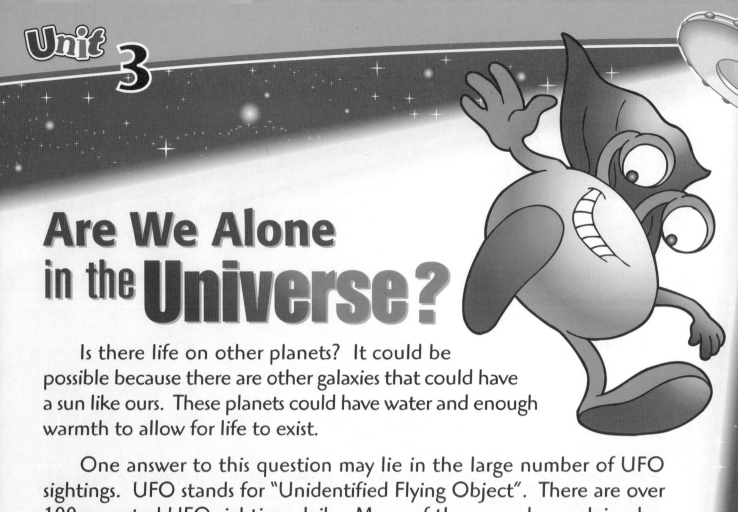

Are We Alone in the Universe?

Is there life on other planets? It could be possible because there are other galaxies that could have a sun like ours. These planets could have water and enough warmth to allow for life to exist.

One answer to this question may lie in the large number of UFO sightings. UFO stands for "Unidentified Flying Object". There are over 100 reported UFO sightings daily. Many of these can be explained as weather balloons, research aircraft, or reflections from the sun. Some scientists believe that many of these sightings are real UFOs. They believe that extraterrestrials (beings from other planets) are trying to visit us or make contact with us.

There are people who believe that they have been captured by aliens. They reported that aliens came to them while they were sleeping and took them into a spaceship. None of them reported being harmed. However, none of these cases have been proven.

Perhaps we are not alone. Perhaps those people who claim to have seen UFOs actually did see them. If so, there will be interesting encounters in space in the future.

ISBN: 978-1-897457-03-0

Remembering Details

A. Fill in the blanks with suitable words.

There could be life on another planet if it has a 1._____ like ours. For life to exist, a planet needs 2._____ and 3._____ . Every day, there are over 4._____ reports from people who think that they have seen an Unidentified Flying Object. A being from another planet is called an 5._____ . These beings would probably travel in 6._____ . Some people believe that they have been 7._____ by aliens but they were not 8._____ .

An Interview with an Alien

> You might use "Who / What / Where / When / Why" to make questions.

B. Pretend that you are interviewing an alien. Write the questions that you want to ask your alien visitor. Then draw the alien.

Question 1. _____

_____

Question 2. _____

_____

Question 3. _____

_____

Question 4. _____

_____

A Picture of My Alien

ISBN: 978-1-897457-03-0

 Adjectives

- **Adjectives** *are words that describe nouns. They tell something about a noun and help us know more about the noun they are describing.*
  Example: *The* <u>playful</u> *kitten jumped up.*
  "Playful" is an adjective that describes the kitten.

C.   Underline the adjectives in the following sentences.

1.   Be careful when crossing a busy street, especially on a slippery road. (3)

The number following each sentence tells how many adjectives are in the sentence.

2.   Wear a warm hat and a winter coat. (2)

3.   Wild animals belong in their natural habitat. (2)

4.   Old Mr. Smith still plays a good round of golf. (2)

5.   The dark night frightened the young children. (2)

 **Using Adjectives**

D.   Fill in the blanks by choosing adjectives that fit the meanings of the sentences.

| excited | birthday | icy | furry | cold | happy | white |

1.   The _____ dog sheds hair on the furniture.

2.   The _____ steps were slippery.

3.   A _____ wind blew as the _____ snow fell.

4.   The _____ child opened her _____ gifts.

5.   We all sang _____ Birthday To You.

ISBN: 978-1-897457-03-0

The Silent "e" and the Long Vowel

- When we add a silent "e" to a word, the vowel in the word changes from short to long.

   Example: The name "Tim", which has the short vowel sound ĭ, changes to the long vowel sound ī in the word "time".
   Notice that this little change also changes the whole meaning of the word. Instead of the name "Tim", we now have the word "time".

E.   Drop the silent "e" in the underlined words. Match the new words with the appropriate meanings.

The Camping Trip

Last summer, our family went camping. We found a spot under a <u>huge</u> <u>pine</u> tree and pitched our tent. After the work, we had a <u>bite</u> to eat. We <u>ate</u> sandwiches and <u>ripe</u> apples. We decided to <u>use</u> the branches of the trees to hang up our towels. We saw a <u>cute</u> chipmunk and watched it <u>hide</u> behind a leaf. We used <u>tape</u> to hang up our garbage bag. We ate an ice <u>cube</u> to cool off. At night we <u>made</u> a <u>fire</u>.

1. slice in two   – _____

2. you and me   – _____

3. just a little, a – _____

4. to tear   – _____

5. touch lightly – _____

6. needle and   – _____

7. shows where – _____

8. angry   – _____

9. a baby bear – _____

10. a type of tree – _____

11. couldn't be seen – _____

12. wrap your arms around – _____

ISBN: 978-1-897457-03-0

SUNFLOWERS

The sunflower plant is a very <u>attractive</u> yellow flower. It gets its name from its yellow sun-like face and also from the ability to <u>rotate</u> its face toward the sun as the sun moves from east to west during the day. With <u>plenty</u> of sun and water, the sunflower can grow over ten feet high.

The sunflower is so <u>pretty</u> that it is often used in flower arrangements. It has been painted by many artists too. Even the <u>famous</u> artist Vincent Van Gogh did a series of sunflower paintings. The sunflower design is often used in arts and crafts and even fabric for clothing.

However, the sunflower is more than a pretty yellow flower. It is an important farm crop and provides food for people and wildlife. Sunflower seeds are used as a snack food. Birds love sunflower seeds and many people buy black oil sunflower seeds for their bird feeders.

The most important use of the sunflower crop is for sunflower oil, which is <u>extracted</u> from sunflower seeds. Sunflower oil is used for salad dressings, frying, and baking.

So you can see that the sunflower is a beautiful plant and also an <u>excellent</u> <u>source</u> of food.

ISBN: 978-1-897457-03-0

Recalling Facts

A. **Circle the correct answer to complete each of the following statements.**

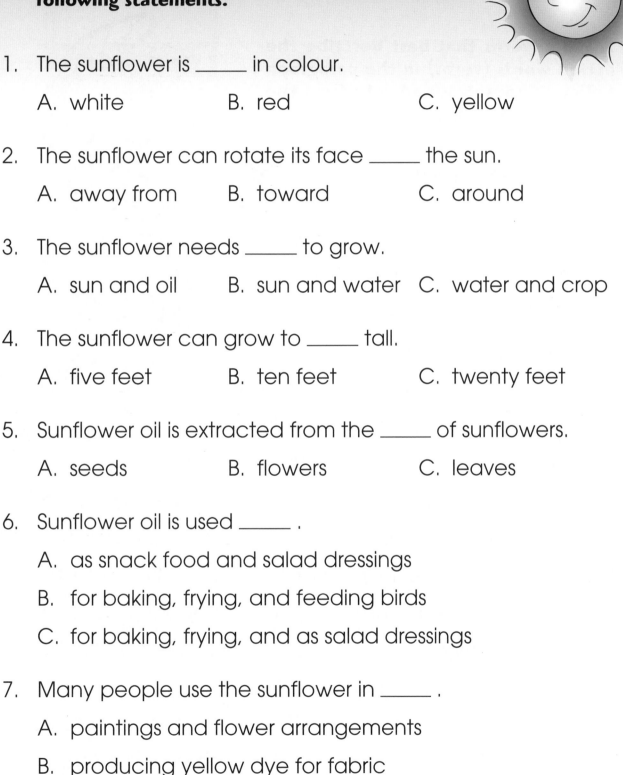

1. The sunflower is _____ in colour.

   A. white   B. red   C. yellow

2. The sunflower can rotate its face _____ the sun.

   A. away from   B. toward   C. around

3. The sunflower needs _____ to grow.

   A. sun and oil   B. sun and water   C. water and crop

4. The sunflower can grow to _____ tall.

   A. five feet   B. ten feet   C. twenty feet

5. Sunflower oil is extracted from the _____ of sunflowers.

   A. seeds   B. flowers   C. leaves

6. Sunflower oil is used _____ .

   A. as snack food and salad dressings

   B. for baking, frying, and feeding birds

   C. for baking, frying, and as salad dressings

7. Many people use the sunflower in _____ .

   A. paintings and flower arrangements

   B. producing yellow dye for fabric

   C. fences and paintings

ISBN: 978-1-897457-03-0

Adverbs

- An **Adverb** describes the verb (action word) in a sentence. It tells something about the verb, such as how an action takes place. Adverbs often end in "ly".

B. Fill in adverbs that best describe the action words (verbs) in the paragraph below. Choose your adverbs from the choices in parentheses.

The Basketball Game

The players leaped (high, low) 1._____ at centre court for the jump ball to start the game. The Raptors player (skilfully, carelessly) 2._____ dribbled the ball past the defensive player. He jumped in the air and shot the ball (directly, nearly) 3._____ at the basket. The ball did not go in and the Grizzlies (noisily, quickly) 4._____ grabbed the rebound. The Raptors player (slowly, cleverly) 5._____ stole the ball from the opposition and ran (swiftly, smartly) 6._____ down the court. The referee blew his whistle (loudly, softly) 7._____ and the play immediately stopped. The fans booed the referee (loudly, quietly) 8._____ when he called a foul on the Raptors player.

ISBN: 978-1-897457-03-0

Crossword Puzzle

C. **Use the underlined words in the passage on page 18 to solve the puzzle.**

Across

A. eye-catching

B. nice-looking

C. where something is obtained

D. very good

Down

1. well-known

2. turn

3. lots of

4. taken out

ISBN: 978-1-897457-03-0

Using Magnets

Magnets are objects that can attract other objects containing iron, steel, or nickel. We can use them in many different ways.

We have all seen how magnetic strips can stick to our fridge at home or a blackboard or whiteboard at school. Fridge magnets come in thousands of designs and many people collect them for fun. They are used for advertising and displaying printed business names and phone numbers. At school, teachers use magnetic strips to hold up signs and magnetic letters for teaching young children.

Magnets are used in toys such as fishing games, building activities, and even board games. Some children have their own horseshoe magnets or a set of bar magnets to play with. These magnets can provide children with lots of fun while they learn about the science of magnetism.

Have you ever noticed how magnets are used to keep windows or doors tightly closed? Since magnets can be made very large and very strong, they are also important in industry. Factories and construction equipment use magnets in their machinery.

A very important use of magnets is for making compasses. A compass is made from a bar magnet that is free to rotate in a case. The magnetic needle in a compass will always point north, so people can use this needle to check their direction. A compass can be a small toy for children or a complicated instrument for a large ship.

As you can see, magnets are used for fun, for building, and for navigation. The use of magnets is a very interesting and important part of our world.

ISBN: 978-1-897457-03-0

 **Recalling Facts**

A. Write "T" for true sentences and "F" for false ones.

1. Sometimes a business will use a magnetic strip to advertise its phone number.   _____

2. Magnets are always small in size.   _____

3. Some people like to collect fridge magnets for fun.   _____

4. A compass is used to check direction.   _____

5. The magnetic needle in a compass will always point towards the west.   _____

6. Children should never use magnets.   _____

B. Describe briefly how magnets are used in the following areas.

1. teaching   : _____

_____

2. business   : _____

_____

3. games   : _____

_____

4. factories   : _____

_____

5. navigation   : _____

_____

ISBN: 978-1-897457-03-0

Pronouns

- **Pronouns** *are words that are used to take the place of nouns.*

Examples:
1. <u>Jennifer</u> was late for school.   <u>She</u> was late for school.
2. <u>Denise and Paula</u> sang a song.   <u>They</u> sang a song.
3. <u>Brian and I</u> went to the store.   <u>We</u> went to the store.
4. Please give this book to <u>Sam</u>.   Please give this book to <u>him</u>.

In each example above, the first underlined word is a noun, and the second is the pronoun replacing the noun.

C. Underline the pronouns in the following sentences.

The number at the end of each sentence tells you how many pronouns to find.

1. Jeff and I went cycling together. (1)

2. He helped him with his homework. (2)

3. The car would not start, so we had it repaired. (2)

4. We saw them running to catch the bus. (2)

5. Alice sent me a message. (1)

D. In each sentence below, choose the correct pronoun to suit the sentence.

1. We / Us _____ are going to walk home together.

2. Me / I _____ like eating popcorn at the movies.

3. Him / He _____ is in my class.

4. She / Her _____ is my best friend.

5. Paul tossed she / me _____ the basketball.

ISBN: 978-1-897457-03-0

Rhyming Words

Some vowels have the same sound even though they are different letters.

E. **Make new words with similar vowel sounds that rhyme. Use the clues to help you.**

1. **kept**

   _____ went slowly

   _____ cried

   _____ went to bed

2. **otter**

   _____ more heat

   _____ goes with "fly"

   _____ Harry's last name

3. **drift**

   _____ a present

   _____ to pick up

   _____ quick or rapid

4. **ore**

   _____ noise when sleeping

   _____ a job around the house

   _____ place to buy candy

5. **cow**

   _____ above your eye

   _____ at this time

   _____ work in the field

6. **giver**

   _____ body part

   _____ flowing water

   _____ shake when cold

7. **chew**

   _____ make coffee

   _____ took to the air

   _____ sticky stuff

8. **feet**

   _____ tidy

   _____ make something hot

   _____ candy

ISBN: 978-1-897457-03-0

There is nothing quite as fun and refreshing as a cool dip in the water on a hot, <u>humid</u> summer day. However, playing in water can be <u>dangerous</u> if you don't know the rules of water safety.

The first <u>rule</u> of water safety is to always swim with a <u>buddy</u>. If you have a problem, the friend can help you or run to get help. Besides, it is always more fun if you have a friend to play with. It is best to have an adult present, especially if you are not a good swimmer. Never swim at a beach where there is no lifeguard or adult present.

Swimming pools are usually well <u>supervised</u> but you can still get injured. Most injuries are a result of children running and slipping on wet pool <u>surfaces</u>. If you are a beginner, always stay in the shallow end.

Water Safety

If you swim in a river or lake, be sure to <u>investigate</u> what is below the water surface. If you jump or dive into unknown waters, you may seriously injure yourself on a hidden object. If you go boating, always wear a life jacket.

Swimming and boating are among the most <u>enjoyable</u> summer activities. Protect yourself by following these basic rules of safety.

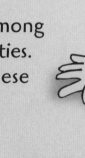

 ISBN: 978-1-897457-03-0

Summarizing Information

A. **In the passage, there are six rules of safety. Write each rule in your own words.**

Rule #1: _____

_____

Rule #2: _____

_____

Rule #3: _____

_____

Rule #4: _____

_____

Rule #5: _____

_____

Rule #6: _____

_____

B. **Pretend that you are a lifeguard at the local swimming pool. Make a sign with important safety rules. Give your sign a catchy title.**

Possessive Nouns

- A **Possessive Noun** shows ownership.
  Example: If John owns a bicycle, you might state:
  This is John's bicycle.
- Note that to show ownership, you add an apostrophe (') and the letter "s".
- Here are three important rules of possessive nouns:
  1. If the noun is singular, add "'s" – The boy's baseball...
  2. If the noun ends in the letter "s", add "'s" – The actress's part in the play...
  3. If the noun is plural, that is, it has an "s" already added to make it plural, add only the apostrophe (') – The horses' hooves could be heard in the distance.

C. **Make the changes needed to make the nouns possessive. Place 's or ' in the spaces provided beside the nouns.**

Example: Here is Paul_____ coat. ⟶ Here is Paul's_____ coat.

1. The little alien_____ neck is very long.

2. These are aliens_____ spaceships.

3. James_____ team won the game.

4. Jim_____ dog followed him to school.

5. They played in the children_____ yard.

6. Julie_____ friend came with her to the game.

7. There is a ladies_____ washroom on the second floor.

8. The coaches_____ whistles blew at the same time.

9. One girl_____ scream could be heard above all the rest.

10. At school, there is a boys_____ washroom on the first floor.

11. The coach was happy with the team_____ performance.

12. The girls_____ cheers were heard throughout the gymnasium.

ISBN: 978-1-897457-03-0

Understanding Words in Sentences

- One way to figure out the meaning of a word is to read the sentence in which the word appears. The information in the sentence will help you understand the meaning of the word.

D. **Find the words listed below in the passage. Match the words in Column A with the meanings in Column B.**

Column A

1. humid ◯
2. dangerous ◯
3. rule ◯
4. buddy ◯
5. supervised ◯
6. surfaces ◯
7. investigate ◯
8. enjoyable ◯

Column B

A. best friend

B. being watched

C. the tops of things

D. hot and sticky weather

E. with lots of fun

F. not very safe

G. thing to obey

H. look into; find out about

Vowels

E. **Answer the questions.**

1. Three words above have four vowels. Can you list these words?

   a. _____   b. _____   c. _____

2. Which word has five vowels? _____

Not all inventions were meant to happen. In some cases, people made mistakes that ended up becoming useful or interesting inventions.

The Popsicle was the result of a mistake. In 1905, an eleven-year-old boy named Frank Epperson was trying to make a flavourful drink. He mixed soda pop powder with water and left it on his back porch overnight. It froze with the stir stick stuck in the middle. The next day he pulled it out and tasted the frozen drink. It was an instant hit. He called it the "Epperson Icicle" and sold them in his neighbourhood for five cents each. He later named the invention "popsicle".

Accidental INVENTIONS

A year before the invention of the popsicle, the ice cream cone was invented. One very hot afternoon at the 1904 St. Louis World's Fair, a young man was selling a lot of ice cream. Soon he ran out of paper ice cream cups. He was desperate to find something in which to serve his ice cream. Then he noticed an Arab vendor selling wafer-like biscuits sprinkled with sugar. He bought a stack of these wafers and put ice cream inside them. He sold his ice cream on the cone-like wafers. This new way to serve ice cream soon became very popular.

Both these cases prove that the old expression "Necessity is the Mother of Invention" is certainly true.

ISBN: 978-1-897457-03-0

Understanding Story Ideas

A. **Write what you think the expression** *"Necessity is the Mother of Invention"* **means.**

Sometimes there is a reason we invent things.

_____

_____

Using Facts to Make Inferences

The term "entrepreneur" refers to a person who comes up with a new business from a good idea or something that he or she invented.

B. **Answer these questions.**

1. Why can we say that Frank Epperson was an "entrepreneur"?

_____

2. How was the invention of the ice cream cone an accident?

_____

3. Are you an inventor? Do you have a great idea for something new? Describe your invention and draw a picture of it.

Name of invention _____

What it is made of _____

What it does _____

Who would use it _____

_____

How much it would
cost _____

ISBN: 978-1-897457-03-0

 Possessive Adjectives

- A **Possessive Adjective** can replace a possessive noun to show ownership.
  Example: This is Jack's cap. This is <u>his</u> cap.

C. Circle the correct possessive adjectives.

1. Michael puts (his / her) toys into the box.

2. Mrs. Smith forgot to bring (her / their) keys.

3. Mom had (its / her) hair permed yesterday.

4. We take (your / our) own lunch to the park.

5. My cat likes licking (their / its) tail.

6. I always have (our / my) breakfast at home.

7. The ducklings follow (their / its) mother to cross the road.

8. I will call you tonight. Can you give me (your / my) telephone number?

D. Fill in the blanks with the suitable possessive adjectives.

my	your	our	their
his	her	its	

1. Have you seen Bob's cat. _____ cat is missing.

2. We all like _____ teacher very much.

3. I am wearing a new dress. Do you like _____ dress?

4. You have a hamster. Is that _____ hamster?

5. I have two brothers. _____ names are Joe and Rob.

6. Fido is the dog's name. _____ name is cute.

ISBN: 978-1-897457-03-0

Digraphs

- **Digraphs** are two letters that, when placed together, make a single sound.
  Examples : 1. rain — the "ai" gives the sound of a long ā.
  play — the "ay" gives the sound of a long ā.

  2. feed — the "ee" gives the sound of a long ē.
  each — the "ea" gives the sound of a long ē.

  3. boat — the "oa" gives the sound of a long ō.

E. Unscramble the mixed-up letters to make proper words.

All of these have digraphs. Put those letters together first and the rest is easy.

1. e r a h c   r e a c h   stretch your arm out

2. t e m e   _ _ _ _   get together with a friend

3. a t m e   _ _ _ _   put it on the barbecue

4. m e t a   _ _ _ _   all the players together

5. o t a c   _ _ _ _   goes with the hat

6. y t a s   _ _ _ _   don't go

7. i s l a   _ _ _ _   you need a boat

8. i t b a   _ _ _ _   you can get hooked on this

9. t y a r s   _ _ _ _ _   sometimes cats or dogs

10. o t s a t   _ _ _ _ _   a quick breakfast

11. e d s e   _ _ _ _   a plant grows from this

ISBN: 978-1-897457-03-0

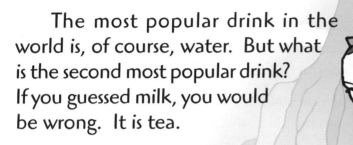

The most popular drink in the world is, of course, water. But what is the second most popular drink? If you guessed milk, you would be wrong. It is tea.

Tea was invented about 4,700 years ago. A Chinese emperor, Shen Nung, was boiling water under a tree when a few leaves fell into his drink. He noticed a pleasant smell coming from the cup. He tasted it, and from that moment on, tea became a drink.

The Second Most
Popular Drink
in the World

Tea became popular in Europe in 1610. Up until about 200 years ago, tea was actually used for money in some Asian countries. People would buy things with a block of tea or carve off a piece of the block for smaller, less expensive purchases.

The most popular form of tea is the tea bag. It was invented by Thomas Sullivan, a tea and coffee merchant. One day, he decided to send samples of tea wrapped in little silk bags to his customers. Much to his surprise, when the orders arrived for his tea, his customers insisted that the tea be wrapped in these little silk bags. The idea of the tea bag was born. Today, more than half the tea in the world is bought this way.

Each year, there are over 800 billion cups of tea consumed worldwide. Perhaps, if Thomas Sullivan hadn't accidentally invented the tea bag, tea would not have been so popular.

ISBN: 978-1-897457-03-0

Choosing Correct Facts

A. **In each group, place a check mark ✔ beside the correct fact. First, answer the questions without looking back at the story. Then, reread the story to check your answers.**

1. A. The most popular drink in the world is water. _____
   B. The most popular drink in the world is tea. _____
   C. The most popular drink in the world is milk. _____

2. A. An emperor of China discovered tea. _____
   B. A queen of England discovered tea. _____
   C. An ancient king discovered tea. _____

3. A. Tea was also used for growing plants. _____
   B. Tea was also used as money. _____
   C. Tea was also used as decoration. _____

4. A. Thomas Sullivan, who invented tea bags, was a merchant. _____
   B. Thomas Sullivan, who invented tea bags, was a sailor. _____
   C. Thomas Sullivan, who invented tea bags, was an explorer. _____

5. A. The first tea bag was made of cloth. _____
   B. The first tea bag was made of paper. _____
   C. The first tea bag was made of silk. _____

6. A. Tea was invented 4,700 years ago. _____
   B. Tea was invented 800 billion years ago. _____
   C. Tea was invented 2,700 years ago. _____

ISBN: 978-1-897457-03-0

Articles

- **A**, **An**, and **The** are articles.

  A is used before a word that begins with a consonant.

  An is used before a word that begins with a vowel.

  The is used before a noun that names a particular person, place, or thing.

B.   Use "a" or "an" before each noun.

1. _____ drink

2. _____ ostrich

3. _____ emperor

4. _____ merchant

5. _____ octopus

6. _____ sample

7. _____ end

8. _____ piece

9. _____ ice cube

10. _____ umbrella

C.   Complete each of the following sentences with "a", "an", or "the".

1. I would like to travel around _____ world.

2. _____ hamburger is the most popular food in America.

3. There is _____ interesting-looking flower in _____ garden.

4. _____ weather today is hot and humid.

5. _____ food in the fridge is still fresh.

6. _____ stranger looked suspicious.

7. Just then, I saw _____ police car pass by.

8. We bought _____ tie for Dad on Father's Day.

ISBN: 978-1-897457-03-0

Consonant Blends

• A **Consonant Blend** is formed when two consonants form a blended sound.

D.   Read the hints. Fill in the blanks with suitable consonant blends.

bl   cl   ch   br   sh   cr   py   tr

1. __ __ e e d after a cut	2. __ __ u e s help solve puzzles
3. __ __ i c k baby chicken	4. s l e e __ __ feeling tired
5. __ __ i c k or treat	6. __ __ a b crawls underwater
7. __ __ i c k for building	8. w a __ __ do with water

E.   Build rhyming words using consonant blends.

beach   walk   fast   lick

1. _____   2. _____   3. _____   4. _____

skim   stay   snore   spill

5. _____   6. _____   7. _____   8. _____

ISBN: 978-1-897457-03-0

Dinosaurs roamed the Earth over 200 million years ago. About 70 million years ago, they completely disappeared. We learn about dinosaurs from fossils. Fossils are found in rocks.

Rocks tell the story of the Earth's history. If we look at the edge of a cliff, we will notice that there are many layers of rock. These layers may be of different colours and thickness. The layers closest to the Earth's surface are the oldest. As time passed, new layers of rock settled on older layers.

Fossils – the Link to the Dinosaur

In between these layers of rock, the skeleton remains of animals were pressed. As years passed and more rock layers piled up, these remains became impressions in the rock. It is these impressions that tell us about the dinosaurs.

The type of rock layer will reveal the time period in the Earth's history. The fossil will show the kind of animal that lived at that time because the skeleton remains were embedded there. From both these facts, we can trace the time period that a certain animal lived. Leaf fossils found in rocks tell us what plants covered the Earth at certain time periods. Therefore, we can also figure out the plant life that the dinosaurs would have depended on for food.

To understand fossils, think of a fresh piece of sidewalk concrete. If you walked on it, you would create the shape of your feet and the length of your step. If thousands of years from now, someone found your footprints in this concrete slab, what would they be able to figure out about you? They would know your shoe size, your height, your weight, and how you walked. This is the same way fossils tell the tale of dinosaurs.

ISBN: 978-1-897457-03-0

The Main Idea of a Paragraph

- **The Main Idea of a Paragraph** is the most important fact or idea that the paragraph tells us.

A. **Place a check mark ✔ in the space beside the statement that tells the main idea of each paragraph from the passage.**

Paragraph One

A. Dinosaurs roamed the Earth. _____

B. We learn about dinosaurs from fossils. _____

C. Dinosaurs are extinct. _____

Paragraph Two

A. Rocks tell the Earth's history. _____

B. The Earth is very rocky. _____

C. There are many layers of rock in a cliff. _____

Paragraph Three

A. Animals were crushed in rocks. _____

B. Many rock layers piled up. _____

C. Skeletal impressions tell about dinosaur history. _____

Paragraph Four

A. Fossils tell us about both plant and animal lives. _____

B. Leaves can be fossils too. _____

C. Dinosaurs ate plants. _____

Paragraph Five

A. Concrete is like a layer of rock. _____

B. Footprints in concrete are like fossils. _____

C. Wet concrete leaves marks. _____

ISBN: 978-1-897457-03-0

Unit 9

The Simple Sentence

- A **Simple Sentence** is made up of a **Subject** and a **Predicate**.

- The **Subject** contains a noun and sometimes an adjective (a word that describes the noun).

- The **Predicate** contains a verb (the action performed by the noun subject) and sometimes an adverb (a word that describes a verb).

  Example: The happy child laughed out loud.

  The subject is "the happy child". The predicate is "laughed out loud".

B. **For each sentence below, draw a line between the subject and the predicate.**

1. The girls played volleyball.

2. His parents went out.

3. They watched television together.

4. The fast runner won the race.

5. The first person in the gym turned on the lights.

C. **Complete the sentences with your own subjects or predicates.**

1. _____ played in the park.

2. _____ were late for school.

3. _____ fed the monkey at the zoo.

4. _____ made some Rice Krispies.

5. The hockey players _____ .

6. The kitten _____ .

7. My father and I _____ .

8. The students in grade three _____ .

40

ISBN: 978-1-897457-03-0

Consonant Blends with Three Letters

- Some **Consonant Blends** are made up of three consonants placed together.

D. Write the three-letter consonant blends to form the words below. Use the clues to help you find the correct words.

1. __ __ __ e a d	put butter on your bread
2. __ __ __ e a m	a small river
3. __ __ __ e a m	a frightful sound
4. __ __ __ e w	tossed the ball
5. __ __ __ a w	use it with a drink
6. __ __ __ a r e	not a circle
7. __ __ __ e e t	where you live
8. __ __ __ i n g	found in a mattress

Triple Consonant Crossword

E. Solve the crossword puzzle.

Across

A. a red fruit
B. a way to cook eggs

Down

1. pull apart
2. wipe clean

Crossword:
- 2 Down: S
- A Across: T _ W _ R Y
- 1 Down: E / T
- B Across: C R _ M B
- B: B

ISBN: 978-1-897457-03-0

True or False

A. **Mark "T" for true and "F" for false in the space provided beside each statement about the information in the passages.**

There are 12 true answers and 13 false ones.

1. Originally Canada was made up of nine provinces and two territories. _____

2. Permafrost means that the ground is always frozen. _____

3. The seal was the most important animal to the Inuit. _____

4. A scientist who studies the universe is called an astronomer. _____

5. We live in a galaxy called the White Way. _____

6. UFO stands for "Unidentified Foreign Object". _____

7. An alien refers to a living being from another planet. _____

8. Warmth and water are needed for a planet to have life. _____

9. The sunflower can grow over 20 feet high. _____

10. The sunflower provides food for people and wildlife. _____

ISBN: 978-1-897457-03-0

11. Magnets can attract other objects containing iron and plastic. _____

12. The magnet in a compass cannot rotate. _____

13. Compasses are only toys for children. _____

14. It is okay to swim at a beach without a lifeguard. _____

15. Pool surfaces are slippery when wet. _____

16. If you are in a small boat, you do not need a life jacket. _____

17. Popsicles were invented in 1975. _____

18. Frank Epperson accidentally invented a popsicle by freezing a drink with a stick in it. _____

19. Ice cream cones were invented at the Olympics in 1904. _____

20. The most popular drink in the world is milk. _____

21. Tea was invented by a Chinese emperor. _____

22. The tea bag is the most popular way that tea is sold today. _____

23. Fossils are impressions in rock. _____

24. The Earth is made up of layers of rock. _____

25. Only animals would leave fossils in rocks. _____

ISBN: 978-1-897457-03-0

Parts of a Sentence

B. There are nouns, pronouns, verbs, adjectives, and adverbs in the following passage. Put the underlined words in the columns under the proper headings.

It <u>was</u> a <u>bright</u>, <u>sunny</u> <u>morning</u> when the students <u>reported</u> to <u>school</u> for the <u>first</u> <u>time</u>. <u>They</u> were all <u>happy</u> to be in school <u>again</u>. They <u>anxiously</u> <u>waited</u> for the first <u>homework</u> assignment. When recess came, they <u>ran</u> <u>quickly</u> out to the huge <u>playground</u>. They <u>picked</u> two equal <u>teams</u> and <u>started</u> a <u>furious</u> game of touch football.

Noun	Pronoun	Verb	Adjective	Adverb
____	____	____	____	____
____	____	____	____	____
____		____	____	____
____		____	____	
____		____	____	
		____		

Adjectives and Adverbs

C. Circle the adjectives and underline the adverbs.

1.	quick	quickly	2.	merrily	merry
3.	smooth	smoothly	4.	rounded	around
5.	nice	nicely	6.	creatively	creative
7.	terribly	terrible	8.	secured	securely

ISBN: 978-1-897457-03-0

Possessive Nouns

D. Rewrite the words to make them possessive.

1. This is the teacher _____ desk.

2. He borrowed Jane _____ pencil.

3. The waitress _____ apron was dirty.

4. The boys _____ washroom is on the first floor.

5. Susie _____ brother is in the first grade.

Possessive Adjectives

E. Write the correct possessive adjectives in the blanks.

1. John hit a home run. It was his / her _____ first big hit.

2. Paul and Jim bought his / their _____ shoes at the same store.

3. We were excited about my / our _____ first trip to Europe.

4. The girl read a story from their / her _____ favourite book.

Articles

F. Circle the correct articles.

1. I have (a / the) cat. (A / The) colour of its hair is white.

2. You need (a / an) apple and (a / an) banana.

3. He wants to travel (a / the) world on (a / an) bike.

4. Can I have (a / an) hot dog and (the / an) ice cream?

ISBN: 978-1-897457-03-0

Simple Sentences

G. **Put each group of words in a sensible order to make a simple sentence. Find the verb first. Look for a noun as the subject of the sentence.**

1. season   is   our   longest   winter

   _____

2. get   seldom   dogs   along   cats   and

   _____

3. into   the   game   overtime   hockey   went

   _____

4. many   how   days   year   school   there   in   are   a

   _____

   _____

H. **Match the subjects in Column A with suitable predicates in Column B.**

Column A

1. The students
2. The figure skater
3. The doctor
4. The roller coaster

Column B

A. saved the man's life

B. listened to the teacher

C. turned everyone upside down

D. slipped and fell

Vowel Sounds

I. **Write "long" or "short" after each word to indicate the vowel sound.**

1. fluke _____

2. luck _____

ISBN: 978-1-897457-03-0

3. truck _____   4. made _____

5. ripe _____   6. ate _____

7. eat _____   8. pin _____

9. needle _____   10. stone _____

Digraphs

> *Digraphs are formed when two letters placed together make a single sound.*

J. Use the same digraphs to make rhyming words.

1. team _____   2. beach _____

3. coat _____   4. pail _____

5. pain _____   6. stay _____

7. roast _____   8. feet _____

Consonants

> *A consonant is any letter that is not a vowel. A consonant blend is formed when two or more consonants placed together make a blended sound.*

K. Complete the words using the meanings given.

1. s l u __ __	wet snow	2. __ __ e a m	thick milk
3. __ __ r e a __	small river	4. __ __ a t	hit a fly
5. __ __ i p	a holiday	6. s __ e a __ __	tricky
7. s __ __ a p	useless piece	8. t e __ __ i b __ e	awful
9. __ __ r o __	toss	10. c h a __ __	tool for writing on the board

ISBN: 978-1-897457-03-0

If you are a superstitious person, you probably believe in bad luck and will do certain things to prevent bad things from happening to you.

Did you know that walking under a ladder was bad luck? This superstition began many years ago when criminals

Are You Superstitious?

were hanged in public. The ladder that led to the scaffold was a symbol of death.

You may see someone knock on wood for good luck. Long ago, it was believed that gods lived in trees and if you knocked on the tree, the god would be happy and take care of you.

Breaking a mirror is supposed to mean seven years of bad luck. This idea came from the belief that the image in the mirror was actually a person's soul. If the mirror broke, the soul would be lost forever.

The day when people are most superstitious is Friday the 13th. The fact that Jesus Christ died on a Friday and that there were 13 men at the Last Supper could be reasons for this belief. Another might be that Friday was called "hangman's day", a day when criminals were executed.

Whether you are superstitious or not shouldn't matter as long as you keep your fingers crossed.

ISBN: 978-1-897457-03-0

Recalling Details

A. Write "T" for true or "F" for false beside each statement.

1. Walking under a ladder is bad luck because something could fall on your head. _____

2. Superstitious people believe in bad luck. _____

3. Long ago, people believed that gods lived in trees. _____

4. Knocking on wood would bring you good luck. _____

5. Breaking a mirror may bring 20 years of bad luck. _____

6. The most superstitious day is the 13th of each month. _____

7. Friday was commonly known as "hangman's day". _____

8. A person's soul was thought to be reflected in a mirror. _____

9. Keeping your fingers crossed is supposed to bring good luck. _____

B. Here are some other well-known superstitions. Can you match them with the beliefs?

Superstition		Belief
1. black cat	◯	A. don't step on it
2. crack in the sidewalk	◯	B. say it after a person sneezes
3. bless you	◯	C. crossing your path brings bad luck

ISBN: 978-1-897457-03-0

Plural Nouns

- *To make a noun plural, usually you can simply add "s". However, some nouns require changes and different plural endings. Here are the rules of plural nouns.*

  1. *Single nouns – just add "s"*
  2. *Nouns ending in "s", "z", "ch", "sh", and "x" – add "es"*
  3. *Nouns ending in "y" – change the "y" to "i" and add "es"*
  4. *Nouns ending in "f" or "fe" – change the "f" or "fe" to "v" and add "es"*
  5. *Nouns ending in "o" – add either "s" or "es" (depending on the word)*
  6. *Some nouns stay the same.*
  7. *Some nouns change in the middle.*

C. **Circle the correct plural forms of the words. State which rules you are following by putting the numbers of the rules.**

Rule

1.	ship	shipes	ships	shipies	
2.	fox	foxes	foxen	foxs	
3.	knife	knives	knifes	knifies	
4.	potato	potatos	potatoes	potatose	
5.	goose	gooses	geeses	geese	
6.	boot	boots	beets	booties	
7.	foot	fots	feet	footies	
8.	half	halfs	halves	halfies	
9.	enemy	enemies	enemys	enemyies	
10.	moose	moose	mooses	meese	

ISBN: 978-1-897457-03-0

Compound Words

- A **Compound Word** is formed when two words are put together to make a new word.

  Example: fire + place = fireplace

D. Match the words from Balloon A with those from Balloon B to make new words. Write your new words in the spaces below.

> Use the clues to figure out the combinations.

A

basket   air
home   over
play   out
photo   night

B

flow   mare
ball   port
ground   work
graph   side

1. _____ a game

2. _____ not in the house

3. _____ swings and things

4. _____ picture this

5. _____ land the jet

6. _____ too full

7. _____ school at home

8. _____ bad dream

> It's a very spooky place.

E. Unscramble the compound word.

G E R A V + R A Y D = __ R __ __ E __ __ R __

ISBN: 978-1-897457-03-0

Babies
of the Arctic

Although the Arctic is a very cold place, there is a variety of wildlife that <u>inhabits</u> the area. The walrus, the seal, and the polar bear are the better-known Arctic animals. Their babies are wrapped in fur or fat to protect them from the bitter cold.

The walrus mother feeds her baby milk for two years. To protect their babies from polar bears and killer whales, walruses stay in groups. When danger <u>appears</u>, they form a circle with their sharp tusks pointing outward to ward off the enemy. No one has ever <u>witnessed</u> a walrus birth but it is <u>believed</u> that the walrus mother gives birth on the ice <u>surface</u> or in the sea. The baby walrus is called a calf.

The seal is only a mother for ten days. Seals leave their pups to take care of themselves. At first, they cry for their mother. When they realize that she is not coming back, they dive into the sea. <u>Immediately</u> they learn how to swim and hunt for food.

Although the polar bear is a big meat-eater, the baby polar bear is born without teeth. The cub cannot see or hear at birth and cannot even walk for a month. Since the cubs do not have enough fur to protect them from the cold, the mother <u>smothers</u> them in her coat and feeds them warm milk. The mother bear must teach the cubs everything necessary for <u>survival</u>.

Remarkably, most of these Arctic babies survive the cold and the danger of <u>predators</u> and grow to <u>adulthood</u> adding to the Arctic animal population.

ISBN: 978-1-897457-03-0

Recalling Details

A. Write short answers for the following questions.

1. How long does the walrus mother feed her babies?

   _____

2. Which Arctic animals are natural enemies of the baby walrus?

   _____

3. How do walruses ward off predators?

   _____

4. How long does the seal take care of her babies?

   _____

5. Why is the polar bear cub considered completely helpless at birth?

   _____

6. What does the mother polar bear do to keep her baby warm?

   _____

7. What natural protection do most Arctic babies have against the cold?

   _____

Your Opinion

B. Answer the question.

   Three dangers that babies of the Arctic face are cold, lack of food, and predators. Which do you think is the worst of these dangers? Give a reason for your choice.

   _____

   _____

ISBN: 978-1-897457-03-0

Unit 11

Subject and Verb Agreement

- When you write a sentence, it is important to have the **Verb (predicate)** agree with the **Noun (subject)**.

- If the subject is singular, the verb must be singular.
  If the subject is plural, the verb must be plural.

C.   Write the proper verb in each of the sentences below.

1.   Good weather (are, is) _____ important when on holiday.

2.   The animals in the forest (was, were) _____ restless.

3.   The students (comes, come) _____ to the gym every week.

4.   Jim and Jackie (is, are) _____ cousins.

5.   Paul (are, is) _____ leaving early.

Tricky Situations

- Words such as "anyone", "each", "everyone", and "no one" always use singular verbs.

- Single words that refer to groups (family, school, team) usually have singular verbs.

D.   Pick the correct verb forms to suit these tricky subjects.

1.   The soccer team (arrives, arrive) _____ today.

2.   The members of the club (is, are) _____ having a meeting.

3.   Everyone (is, are) _____ coming to the party.

4.   Each of the boys (comes, come) _____ by car.

5.   The school (was, were) _____ getting together to raise money.

ISBN: 978-1-897457-03-0

New Words: Building Vocabulary

E. Match the ten underlined words in the reading passage with the meanings.

Underlined Word	Meaning
1. inhabits	A. right away
2. appears	B. thought it was true
3. witnessed	C. the top of something
4. believed	D. going on living
5. surface	E. covers completely
6. immediately	F. hunters
7. smothers	G. saw it happen
8. survival	H. lives there
9. predators	I. grown-ups
10. adulthood	J. comes into view

F. Create new words from these words by adding new beginnings or endings.

1. survival + ing = _____

2. believed + able = _____

3. appears + ance = _____

4. inhabited + un = _____

 ISBN: 978-1-897457-03-0

Trick or Treat

On Halloween Night, children go trick-or-treating in their neighbourhoods. Dressed up as ghosts, skeletons, devils, and various other characters, children knock on doors to collect their treats. Seldom do they actually perform a "trick".

It is thought that trick-or-treating comes from an old English custom. On All Souls Day, poor people went begging and promised to say prayers in exchange for food. Apple bobbing, still a favourite Halloween game, was originally an ancient ceremony honouring harvest time.

A jack-o'-lantern is placed on porches and windows to tell children that treats are available. The legend has it that a man named Jack couldn't enter heaven because he played tricks on the devil. As punishment, he had to wander the Earth carrying a lantern waiting to be judged fit to get into heaven.

People believed that Halloween marked the connection between the world of the living and the world of the dead. This meant that ghosts would roam the Earth on this night. Some believed that these ghosts would go back to the homes they lived in before they died.

Thankfully, Halloween is a fun night when children can dress up and get a bag full of candy. We don't have to worry about ghosts. Or do we?

ISBN 978-1-897457-03-0

Matching Facts

A. Match the facts from Column A with the meanings in Column B.

| **Column A** | **Column B** |

1. trick-or-treating   _____

2. apple bobbing   _____

3. jack-o'-lantern   _____

4. Jack   _____

5. All Souls Day   _____

A. shows that treats are available

B. old English custom

C. people went begging

D. honours harvest time

E. wanders the Earth

B. Write short answers for the following questions.

1. Why did Jack have to wander the Earth?

_____

_____

2. Why did ghosts roam the Earth on Halloween?

_____

_____

3. How do children know where they can collect treats?

_____

_____

_____

ISBN: 978-1-897457-03-0

Verb Tenses

- Verbs change according to which time period they are in.

  Examples: I walk. I am walking. – **Present Time**

  I walked. I did walk. I was walking. I have walked. – **Past Time**

  I will walk. I shall walk. – **Future Time**

C.   Write the missing verb tenses in the chart below.

	Present	Past	Future
1.	carry		
2.		ran	
3.	think		
4.			will fight
5.	try		
6.			will swim

D.   Fill in the blanks with the proper form of the verbs in parentheses.

1. Jim (play) _____ basketball yesterday.

2. Susan (try) _____ to help you tomorrow.

3. The students (work) _____ on their projects for two days.

4. Paul and Peter (fly) _____ the kite when the wind comes up.

5. She (walk) _____ home with her friends every day.

6. His parents (take) _____ a holiday next summer.

7. He usually (go) _____ shopping on weekends.

8. I (meet) _____ Jason this morning on my way to school.

ISBN: 978-1-897457-03-0

Halloween Words

E. **Here are some familiar Halloween words. Write a Halloween story using some of these words.**

You might want to tell about a scary Halloween night that you remember. Draw a picture of your favourite Halloween costume in the box.

ghosts   scary   windy   shadows   noises   candy
skeletons   graveyard   dark   witches   bats   moon
pumpkin   screams   chills   costumes   goblins   masks

ISBN: 978-1-897457-03-0

Hamburger –
the Most Popular American Food

When was the last time you had a hamburger? Was there any ham in it? The word "hamburger" looks like a combination of the words "ham" and "burger". Therefore, one would naturally think that a hamburger means a burger with ham. But why is the hamburger called "hamburger" when there is no ham in it?

The word "hamburger" has nothing to do with ham. In fact, it comes from the seaport city – Hamburg in Germany. In the 1700s, during the time of American settlement, a lot of European immigrants moved to the New World. At that time, the port of Hamburg was the last piece of European soil the immigrants felt under their feet before their voyage to the unknown. Hamburger was a food that the European immigrants had on board the Hamburg-America Line.

Like the Italian immigrants that brought the pizza to America, the German immigrants brought in the hamburger. It became even more popular with the opening of the numerous fast food restaurant chains in America and all over the world. Strangely, though, the Germans did not use the name "hamburger" in their mother tongue. In German, it was called "frikadelle". Somehow, the word "hamburger" reminded them of their voyage and their homeland.

ISBN: 978-1-897457-03-0

 **Recalling Facts**

A. Circle the correct answers.

1. Hamburg is the name of a ____ .

   A. town   B. port   C. food

2. The New World refers to ____ .

   A. America   B. Europe   C. Italy

3. The early immigrants to the New World travelled by ____ .

   A. ship   B. boat   C. railroad

4. Pizzas were brought to America by the ____ .

   A. Canadians   B. Germans   C. Italians

5. "Hamburger" reminded the immigrants of their ____ .

   A. forefathers   B. early days in the New World
   C. homeland

6. "Frikadelle" is a/an ____ word.

   A. German   B. American   C. Italian

EXtra Workout

B.

Can you think of the name of another food that is as misleading as "hamburger"?

_____

ISBN: 978-1-897457-03-0

Capitalization

- Here are some rules of **Capitalization**:
  1. Use a capital letter to begin a sentence.
  2. Use a capital letter for names (people, pets).
  3. Use a capital for the names of places on the map (cities, lakes, rivers, countries...).
  4. Use a capital for names of places and things such as buildings, companies, and historic sites.
  5. Use a capital for days of the week and months of the year.
  6. Use a capital for titles (Dr., Mr., Mrs., Miss, Ms., Prime Minister, President, Professor, Prince, Queen...).
  7. Use capitals for the words in titles of books, movies, and songs (even your own stories).

C. **There are 33 missing capitals in the story below. Write over the letters that should be capitalized in dark pen or pencil.**

You be the teacher. Correct the words.

my trip to england

my name is billy henderson. i live at 723 main st. my dad is a doctor and his patients call him dr. henderson. this summer we are going on a holiday to england to visit my aunt, rita. rita lives near the thames river. we are going to visit buckingham palace while we are there. our flight is booked on british airways and we will land at heathrow airport. we are leaving on august 11, and returning on september 3. while we are away, our neighbour, mrs. watson, will look after our dog, scamp.

ISBN: 978-1-897457-03-0

Building Vocabulary

D. Fill in each blank with a suitable word from the passage.

1. Spanish is Mark's mother _____ .

2. The early _____ mainly came from Europe.

3. The _____ to the New World was filled with danger.

4. There were a lot of people on _____ the ship.

5. "Homeland" is a _____ of
   the words "home" and "land".

E. Create compound words with the words in the apples in the tree.

board

paper

ship

coat

wood

print

1. space_____

2. news_____

3. finger_____

4. black_____

5. rain_____

6. fire_____

A compound word is formed when two words are put together to make a new word.

ISBN: 978-1-897457-03-0

Next time your friend tells you not to chew gum, you could say that you are exercising your jaw. That's the reason a dentist named William Semple invented gum in 1869. But his gum was not a big success because it was flavourless. People preferred to chew the gum from the spruce tree because it had a pleasant taste.

Spruce gum was scarce because spruce trees were being cut down to make paper. Later, Thomas Adams combined chicle, a rubbery sap from the sapodilla tree of

The Origin of Gum Chewing

South America, with gum to create a new flavour sensation. In 1871, Adams invented a machine that made chicle gum into sticks. He claimed that his gum could improve blood circulation, strengthen teeth, and refresh the brain.

Soon, candy-coated gum named "little chicles" came along, which became known as "Chiclets". Following the invention of Chiclets was Blibber-Blubber. It was a strong form of gum that enabled the chewer to blow bubbles. Soon, people around the world started chewing gum.

For years, students have been hiding their gum under their desks to prevent being caught chewing gum in class. An even quicker way of getting rid of the evidence is to swallow it! This may make the gum disappear quickly but it is not a good idea because gum never really gets digested properly.

ISBN: 978-1-897457-03-0

Comprehension Crossword Puzzle

A. Solve the crossword puzzle using words from the story, "The Origin of Gum Chewing".

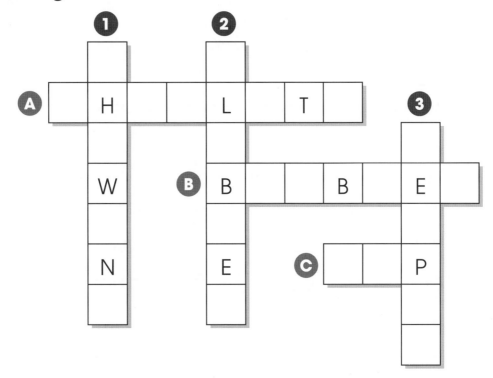

Across

A. candy-coated gum

B. what you can blow

C. Chicle is a rubbery form of this.

Down

1. exercising with gum

2. goes with Blubber

3. William's other name

Your Opinion

B. Give two reasons why you think chewing gum is so popular throughout the world.

1. _____

2. _____

ISBN: 978-1-897457-03-0

Contractions

- **Contractions** are single words that are formed by combining and shortening two words.

  Examples: can + not = cannot ⟶ can't

                I + will   = I'll

  Note the use of the apostrophe to replace letters.

C. Form contractions from the following pairs of words.

1. she will   = _____
2. he had   = _____

3. we are   = _____
4. you are   = _____

5. were not = _____
6. who is   = _____

7. did not   = _____
8. has not   = _____

9. I am   = _____
10. that is   = _____

11. have not = _____
12. would not = _____

13. is not   = _____
14. there is   = _____

Be Creative

You may write about gum chewing.

D. Use five of the contractions to make sentences of your own.

1. _____

2. _____

3. _____

4. _____

5. _____

ISBN: 978-1-897457-03-0

Homonyms

- **Homonyms** are words that sound the same but are spelled differently.
  Example: hear   here
                I could not <u>hear</u> what he said.   He was <u>here</u> on time.

E.   Read each sentence and select the correct homonym to suit the meaning.

Use a dictionary if you are not sure which word to use.

1. He has bean / been _____ to school every day.

2. My son / sun _____ works downtown.

3. I would / wood _____ like to travel.

4. When she was ill, she looked pale / pail _____ .

5. All weak / week _____ we have to go to school.

6. The hair / hare _____ beat the tortoise in a race.

7. I couldn't stop my bicycle because the brake / break _____ didn't work.

8. The cake was made out of flower / flour _____ .

9. The made / maid _____ cleaned the hotel room.

10. We had to weight / wait _____ in line.

11. The turtle fell into the hole / whole _____ .

12. You should write / right _____ the answer in the box.

ISBN: 978-1-897457-03-0

A simple garden shows how a food chain works. Suppose you have lettuce growing in your garden. That lettuce gets energy from sunlight. It also soaks up water and nutrients from the soil. It now has everything it needs to grow. Think of this lettuce as the first link in a garden food chain.

Suppose one night a slug slithers onto the leaf of the lettuce and begins eating it. The energy from the lettuce is now transferred to the slug. The slug becomes the second link in the food chain. In the morning, a beetle comes along and eats the slug. The energy from the slug is now passed on to the beetle, which becomes the third link in the chain.

Just then, along comes a hungry shrew that eats the beetle. Now the shrew is enjoying all the energy in the chain. But the food chain is not over. A wise old owl swoops down, picks up the shrew, and returns to its nest to prepare it for dinner.

The Food Chain

The owl has no natural predators. That means that there is no animal that tries to kill the owl for food. The owl is at the top of this food chain and benefits from all the energy passed through all the members of the chain – the lettuce, the slug, the beetle, and the shrew.

There are many different food chains in nature. Each environment has its own food chain. We, too, are part of a food chain. Lucky for us, like the wise old owl, we are also at the top of our chain.

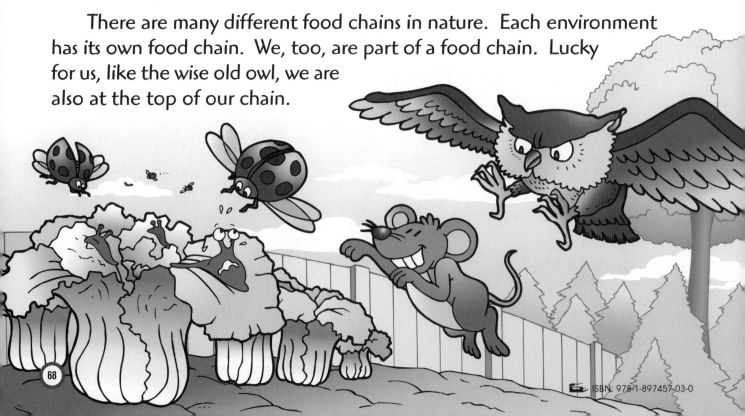

ISBN: 978-1-897457-03-0

Understanding Facts

A.   Put the members of this food chain in order.

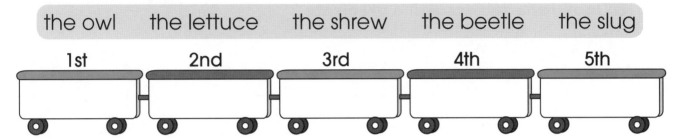

the owl   the lettuce   the shrew   the beetle   the slug

| 1st | 2nd | 3rd | 4th | 5th |

Understanding Information

B.   Answer the following questions about the food chain.

1.   In the food chain, what is the role of the sun and the nutrients in the soil?

_____

_____

2.   What does it mean to transfer energy?

_____

_____

3.   Why do you think that the owl has no natural predators?

_____

_____

4.   If we are part of a food chain, what position in the chain would we be placed?

_____

5.   Can you name three animals that would be at the top of their food chains? (not from the reading passage)

a. _____   b. _____   c. _____

ISBN: 978-1-897457-03-0

 Creating Simple Sentences

C. **Unscramble each group of words to make a proper sentence. Remember to look for a subject and a predicate.**

1. game   the   we   won

   _____

2. long   it   day   rained   all

   _____

3. cream   ice   he   two   ate   scoops   of

   _____

4. holidays   summer   finally   here   are

   _____

5. the   test   gave   teacher   students   a   the

   _____

6. water   the   up   plants   soil   from   soak   the

   _____

D. **Match the subjects with the suitable predicates.**

Subject

1. The old man
2. The crying baby
3. The policeman
4. All the students

Predicate

A. gathered in the school gymnasium
B. walked with a cane
C. made a lot of noise
D. chased the thief

ISBN: 978-1-897457-03-0

Synonyms

- A **Synonym** is a word that means the same as another word.

E. Complete the crossword puzzle with words that match the clues.

Try to match the synonyms in the word bank with the clue words first.

Across

A. sad
B. oceans
C. total
D. remain
E. finish

Down

1. cut
2. rude
3. dish
4. lower

plate   stay   end   saw
unhappy   drop   nasty
add   seas

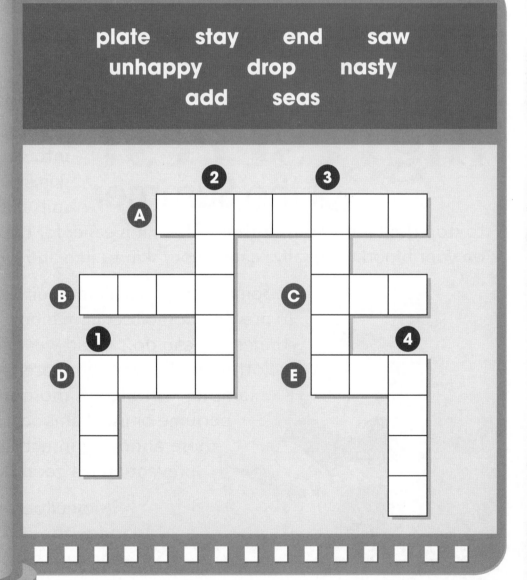

ISBN: 978-1-897457-03-0

Most people would agree that summer's biggest pest is the mosquito. This pesky little insect can quickly ruin a walk in the woods or a holiday at a cottage.

Actually, only the female mosquito bites. The male mosquito feeds on plant juices. The female mosquito drinks our blood to get protein needed to make eggs. One bite into your arm or leg can help the female mosquito produce 50 to 100 eggs.

The Biggest Pest
of the Summer

The mosquito has a pointed beak that sticks into your skin. Once your skin is pierced, the mosquito spits saliva into the wound to stop the blood from clotting. Then, it is easier for the mosquito to fill up on your blood. The saliva causes your skin to itch and swell up.

Some people attract mosquitoes more than others. To prevent mosquitoes from biting you, there are some things you can do. Avoid wearing dark colours and clothes made of rough materials. Blue jeans, for example, will attract mosquitoes. Don't wear perfume or use shampoo. These scents attract these annoying insects. Probably the best prevention is a good insect repellent.

Mosquitoes are very sneaky. They land without a sound and weigh almost nothing. You usually notice them only after they have already enjoyed a meal of your blood.

ISBN: 978-1-897457-03-0

Checking Facts

A. Write "T" for true and "F" for false in the space provided beside each statement.

1. Only the male mosquito bites people. _____

2. Mosquitoes spit saliva into the wound from the bite. _____

3. The saliva in the wound stops blood from clotting. _____

4. There is seldom an itch after a bite. _____

5. The mosquito's saliva can stop bleeding. _____

6. All people attract mosquitoes the same. _____

7. Light coloured clothes attract mosquitoes. _____

8. Blue jeans attract mosquitoes. _____

9. Mosquitoes do not like perfume and shampoo. _____

10. Mosquitoes are noisy. _____

11. Mosquitoes are very light. _____

12. One mosquito can produce 50 to 100 eggs. _____

Using Information

B. Answer the questions.

1. Imagine you are at a cottage in the middle of mosquito season. What would you do to protect yourself?

_____

_____

2. Explain how the mosquito sucks blood.

_____

_____

ISBN: 978-1-897457-03-0

Building Sentences with Adverbs and Adjectives

- Remember that an **Adjective** describes a noun and an **Adverb** describes a verb. We use adjectives and adverbs to give more information and make sentences more interesting.

C. Rewrite the following sentences with the adjectives and adverbs provided. Add <u>both</u> words to each sentence.

1. The boy ran. (happy, quickly)

   _____

2. The wind blew. (howling, furiously)

   _____

3. The students sang the songs. (talented, loudly)

   _____

4. The game was finished. (exciting, early)

   _____

5. John, the boy in the class, was late. (tallest, again)

   _____

D. Add your own descriptive words to the story below.

The 1._____ girl received a 2._____ bicycle for her birthday. She was very 3._____ to get such a 4._____ gift. She rode 5._____ down the road towards the 6._____ house of her 7._____ friend, Sarah. It was a very 8._____ day for her.

ISBN: 978-1-897457-03-0

Antonyms

- An **Antonym** is a word that has the opposite meaning of another word.

E. Solve the antonym word puzzles. Unscramble the antonyms and place the answers in the boxes.

1.	m e n y e	☐☐☐☐☐	friend
2.	l a y p	☐☐☐☐	work
3.	e f a s	☐☐☐☐	dangerous
4.	d r a h	☐☐☐☐	soft
5.	m a c l	☐☐☐☐	windy
6.	u n i r	☐☐☐☐	repair
7.	p m e y t	☐☐☐☐☐	crowded
8.	k e a w	☐☐☐☐	strong

F. Circle the antonym for each word from the choices.

1. beautiful	ugly	happy	careful	pretty
2. funny	joking	comical	serious	laughing
3. unusual	regular	peculiar	odd	strange
4. exciting	interesting	dull	fun	scary
5. tame	soft	gentle	wild	rare

ISBN: 978-1-897457-03-0

Before winter arrives, many species of birds instinctively know that it's time to head south. The mystery of migration has always puzzled us. Why do only some birds migrate? How do birds know when to go south? How do they find their way?

Some birds fly south because their food supply runs short in winter. The woodpecker, for example, does not need to fly south because it can find food stuck in the bark of trees. The insects that the woodpecker eats are safe in the bark from the winter cold and snow.

Some birds rely on grains, shoots, insects, and other foods that disappear in winter. These birds must head south where food is still available. But why do they not stay south? Perhaps they know that if they stayed down south, they would run out of food there, too.

It is possible that birds know when winter is coming because they notice that the days are getting shorter. Once they leave from the north, they use the sun as a compass. The sun is in different positions in the sky at various times of day. In order to use it as a guide, birds would have to know the time of day. On long flights, birds use the stars to navigate their route.

The Mystery of Migration

The homing pigeon does not use the sun or the stars. Scientists believe that it uses the magnetic field of the Earth. One of the most amazing migrations is that of the tiny hummingbird. It travels from Canada to Mexico – a distance of over 3,200 kilometres.

ISBN 978-1-897457030-8

Choosing Correct Facts

A. **Place a check mark ✔ in the space beside the answer that makes the correct statement.**

1. Birds know when to fly south because
   A. they see the sunrise.   _____
   B. they have good instincts.   _____
   C. they follow a leader.   _____

2. It is believed that birds fly south because
   A. they need food.   _____
   B. they like warm weather.   _____
   C. they get lost.   _____

3. The woodpecker does not need to fly south because
   A. it has no instincts.   _____
   B. its food is protected in the bark of trees.   _____
   C. it does not know the way.   _____

4. Birds do not stay south because
   A. they get too warm.   _____
   B. they follow the sun.   _____
   C. they do not want the food supply to run out there.   _____

5. On long migration flights, birds navigate by
   A. the stars.   _____
   B. other birds.   _____
   C. the weather.   _____

6. The homing pigeon is different because it finds its way by
   A. following the sun.   _____
   B. using the magnetic field of the Earth.   _____
   C. following the same route.   _____

ISBN 978-1-897457-03-0

Unit 17

Types of Sentences

- **Sentences** are written for different purposes.
  1. An **Interrogative Sentence** asks a question.
     Example: What time is it? (A question mark follows an interrogative sentence.)
  2. A **Declarative Sentence** makes a simple statement.
     Example: The boy walked his dog. (A period ends a declarative sentence.)
  3. An **Exclamatory Sentence** shows emotion.
     Example: Look out for the car! (An exclamatory sentence is followed by an exclamation mark.)
  4. An **Imperative Sentence** tells what you want to happen.
     Example: Wait until you're called. (An imperative sentence is followed by a period.)

B. **Punctuate each sentence and state the type of sentence (interrogative, declarative, imperative, exclamatory) in the space provided.**

At the Baseball Game

At a professional baseball game, exciting things happen.

1. Take your seats before the game begins _____

2. Which team is winning so far _____

3. The bases are loaded _____

4. Wow, what a great catch _____

5. Is the runner fast enough to steal a base _____

C. **Pretend you are at the game. Make up four sentences about the game.**

1. Interrogative _____

2. Declarative _____

3. Imperative _____

4. Exclamatory _____

ISBN: 978-1-897457-03-0

Idioms

- An **Idiom** is a group of words that has a meaning other than what it really says.

- We use idioms today to get ideas across. Idioms are convenient because they are widely known and understood.

D. Here are some everyday idioms. Can you guess what they mean? Write explanations in the spaces provided.

1. "The early bird catches the worm."

   _____

2. He led me on a "wild goose chase".

   _____

3. We tried to "butter up" the teacher to get less homework.

   _____

4. When she lost her cat, she "was feeling blue".

   _____

5. The students were "in hot water" over the broken window.

   _____

6. My dad "blew his top" when he got a flat tire.

   _____

E. Write sentences using these idioms.

1. out of this world _____

2. spill the beans _____

3. going bananas _____

ISBN: 978-1-897457-03-0

Mary - Kate and Ashley Olsen

The twin sisters, Mary-Kate and Ashley Olsen, are two of the most popular television, film, and music stars in North America. They became the youngest self-made millionaires in American history before they were 10 years old.

Born on June 13, 1986 in Los Angeles, California, Mary-Kate is two minutes younger than Ashley. They have a brother named Trent and a sister named Elizabeth. Both Trent and Elizabeth sometimes appear in their videos.

From the age of 9 months until the age of 9 years, they shared the role of Michelle Tanner on the hit series, "Full House". Since the producers did not want the public to know that Michelle was played by the twins, they were credited as Mary Kate Ashley Olsen in its early seasons.

The "Our First Video" production of theirs was No. 1 on the Billboard chart and remained on top for 12 weeks. It stayed in the top 10 for 157 weeks. All this was accomplished when they were only 7 years old!

Although Mary-Kate and Ashley are famous, they are very ordinary. They like to shop, sing and act, dance, and watch music videos. When they were little, they only received $10.00 a week for allowance.

ISBN: 978-1-897457-03-0

Remembering Details

A. Fill in the blanks.

> "Full House" nine months Trent
>
> ten dollars Michelle Tanner younger
>
> California "Our First Video" Elizabeth

1. Mary-Kate and Ashley starred in a television show when they were _____ old.

2. They have a brother named _____ and a sister named _____ .

3. Mary-Kate is _____ than Ashley.

4. Their first television show was called _____ .

5. When they were young, they shared the role of _____ in their first television show.

6. The twin sisters earned a lot of money in television but they only got _____ a week for allowance when they were younger.

7. Their No. 1 video was called _____ .

8. They were born in the state of _____ .

ISBN: 978-1-897457-03-0

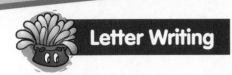 **Letter Writing**

B. Write a letter to Mary-Kate and Ashley Olsen.

> *Think of 3 or 4 questions you might ask them. Try to write complete sentences with descriptive words. Tell them something about you: where you live, your family members, the name of your school, your hobbies, your pet's name…*

_____ Date

Dear Mary-Kate and Ashley,

All about yourself here

_____
_____
_____
_____
_____

Ask questions about them here

_____
_____
_____
_____

Closing remark

_____
_____

Yours truly,

_____
Your name

ISBN: 978-1-897457-03-0

Building New Words

- **New Words** are built from root words.
  Example: true → *untrue truly truth*

C. Circle the words in the word search.

happiness
harmful
finest
newest
pitiful
priceless
eventful
trapped
tossing
sadness
stopper
building

b	u	i	l	d	i	n	g	j	k
h	a	r	m	f	u	l	q	w	e
a	s	m	p	i	t	i	f	u	l
p	a	f	t	n	e	w	e	s	t
p	r	i	c	e	l	e	s	s	r
i	r	t	o	s	s	i	n	g	a
n	o	n	h	t	r	v	u	l	p
e	v	e	n	t	f	u	l	z	p
s	e	s	a	d	n	e	s	s	e
s	n	s	t	o	p	p	e	r	d

D. Write out the root word of each of the words in (C).

ISBN: 978-1-897457-03-0

Recalling Facts

A. Circle the best choice for each sentence.

1. The ladder that led to the hanging scaffold was a symbol of
   A. bad luck.   B. death.   C. good luck.

2. Breaking a mirror means seven years of
   A. hard times.   B. being poor.   C. hard luck.

3. People are most superstitious about
   A. Halloween.   B. Friday the 13th.
   C. New Year's Eve.

4. Many Arctic baby animals are kept warm by
   A. fire.   B. the sun.   C. fur or fat.

5. A baby seal is called a
   A. calf.   B. pup.   C. cub.

6. Trick-or-treating is an old custom from
   A. England.   B. Spain.   C. Germany.

7. Today, a jack-o'-lantern on a porch means that
   A. candy is available.   B. beware of ghosts.
   C. nobody's home.

8. In the old days, on All Souls Day poor people went
   A. trick-or-treating.   B. begging for food.
   C. to church.

9. Hamburg is a city in
   A. America.   B. Italy.   C. Germany.

10. At first, gum was not a big success because it was
    A. too sticky.   B. flavourless.   C. too rubbery.

ISBN: 978-1-897457-03-0

11. In 1871 Adams invented a machine to turn gum into
    A. candy. B. sticks. C. bubble gum.

12. The last link in a food chain has no
    A. growth. B. natural enemies.
    C. way to get food.

13. The male mosquito feeds on
    A. human blood. B. other mosquitoes.
    C. plant juices.

14. The saliva placed in the bite by the mosquito prevents
    A. itching. B. swelling. C. blood clotting.

15. To avoid being bitten by a mosquito, avoid wearing
    A. dark colours. B. light colours. C. colourful clothing.

16. To know when to head south, birds rely on
    A. other birds. B. instinct. C. their memory.

17. The woodpecker does not have to fly south because
    A. its food is protected in a tree.
    B. it doesn't get cold.
    C. it has no instincts.

18. The homing pigeon is probably guided by
    A. the sounds of other birds.
    B. the magnetic field of the Earth.
    C. the stars.

19. From the age of 9 months to 9 years, Mary-Kate and Ashley
    starred in the television show
    A. "Full House". B. "Fun Place". C. "Our House".

20. Mary-Kate and Ashley were born in
    A. 1986. B. 1990. C. 1980.

ISBN: 978-1-897457-03-0

Plural Nouns

B.   Write the plural form of the following nouns.

1. ship		2. potato	
3. foot		4. knife	
5. fox		6. half	
7. wife		8. deer	

Subject and Verb Agreement

C.   Place the correct form of the verbs in the spaces provided.

1.   John and Phillip (is, are) _____ in the same class.

2.   We (were, was) _____ happy to see them.

3.   The children (go, goes) _____ to their classrooms.

4.   They (take, takes) _____ a break for lunch.

5.   The fish (are, is) _____ swimming in the same direction.

Verb Tenses

D.   Change the verb tenses to suit the sense of the sentences.

1.   He (arrive) _____ home tomorrow.

2.   I (walk) _____ a long way yesterday.

3.   The dog (jump) _____ over the fence when its master commands.

4.   The men (work) _____ on the bridge all of last week.

ISBN: 978-1-897457-03-0

Capitalization

E. In the following sentences, place capital letters over the small letters that should be capitalized.

1. mr. jones was also known as dr. jones when he was at toronto general hospital.

2. linda and lauren attended willow avenue public school.

3. they took a canoe trip on the niagara river near quebec city.

4. we all read the harry potter books by j.k. rowling.

Contractions

F. Change the following words to contraction form.

1. she will		2. we will	
3. did not		4. have not	
5. would not		6. that is	

Types of Sentences

G. Place the name of the type of sentence (declarative, interrogative, imperative, exclamatory) in each space below. Punctuate each sentence.

1. How are you feeling today _____

2. Today is Monday _____

3. Look out _____

4. Sit down and be quiet _____

ISBN: 978-1-897457-03-0

Homonyms

 *Homonyms are words that sound the same but are spelled differently.*

H. Write the homonym of each word by unscrambling the letters.

1. made — d i a m — [_____]

2. hire — h g r e i h — [_____]

3. break — k a e b r — [_____]

4. pear — r i a p — [_____]

Synonyms

 *Synonyms are words that mean the same as other words.*

I. In each group, underline the word that is not a synonym for the one on the left.

1. **unhappy**	miserable	joyous	upset
2. **creative**	smart	dull	imaginative
3. **swift**	quick	fast	smooth
4. **powerful**	proud	strong	muscular
5. **careful**	slow	cautious	attentive

 Antonyms

 *Antonyms are words that are opposite of other words.*

J. In each group, underline the word that is an antonym for the one on the left.

1. **friendly**	nice	happy	rude
2. **crowded**	empty	populated	full
3. **rough**	smooth	plain	rugged
4. **wet**	soaked	dry	drenched
5. **hurt**	injured	wounded	healthy

ISBN: 978-1-897457-03-0

Compound Words

89

K. **Match the words that make good compound word combinations. Write the compound words.**

Group A

fire	straw	photo
base	bath	fore
hand	note	pillow
grape	out	down
news	every	mail

Group B

room	ball	place
head	writing	berry
graph	fruit	book
town	body	box
side	case	paper

1. _____   2. _____   3. _____

4. _____   5. _____   6. _____

7. _____   8. _____   9. _____

10. _____   11. _____   12. _____

13. _____   14. _____   15. _____

New Words

L. **Match the new words with the definitions.**

1. inhabits ⟶ ◯   A. hunters

2. witnessed ⟶ ◯   B. instantly

3. predators ⟶ ◯   C. grown up

4. immediately ⟶ ◯   D. saw it happen

5. adulthood ⟶ ◯   E. lives in

ISBN: 978-1-897457-03-0

ISBN: 978-1-897457-03-0

Outside

Inside

ISBN: 978-1-897457-03-0

Common Nouns

A **common noun** is the general term for a person, an animal, a place, or a thing.

Examples: person – teacher, brother, driver, friend
                animal – cat, dog, bear, bird
                place – home, school, playground, shop
                thing – book, bus, toy, hamburger

A. Write the nouns on the correct balloons.

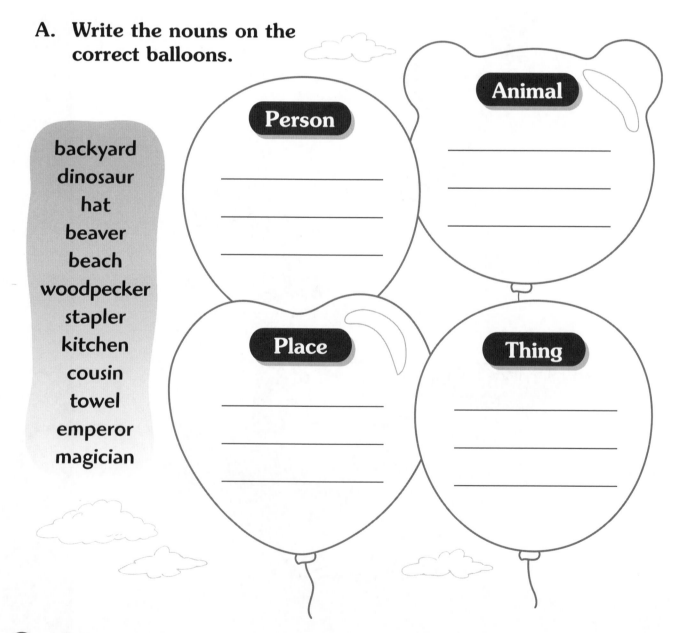

backyard
dinosaur
hat
beaver
beach
woodpecker
stapler
kitchen
cousin
towel
emperor
magician

Person

Animal

Place

Thing

ISBN: 978-1-897457-03-0

Proper Nouns

A **proper noun** is a name for a specific person, animal, place, or thing. It always begins with a capital letter.

Examples: Peter, Golden Retriever, CN Tower, Toronto Star

B. Fill in the blanks with the given words. Use capital letters for proper nouns.

north america	pen pal	winter	kelly
australia	benjamin	basketball	yahoo
country	chris bosh	hobbies	raptors

Dear 1._____ ,

　　How are you? My name is 2._____ . I'm eight years old. I saw your advertisement on 3._____ and would like to be your 4._____ . I live in Canada, which is in 5._____ . It is very cold in 6._____ here. How about you in 7._____ ? Is it cold there?

　　I like playing 8._____ . I usually play it with my dad. My favourite team is the 9._____ and my favourite player is 10._____ . What are your 11._____ ? Please reply and tell me about you and your 12._____ .

Best wishes,

Benjamin

Plural Nouns

A **plural noun** is a name referring to more than one person or thing.
We can make a noun plural by adding "s", but for nouns

- ending in "s", "z", "ch", "sh", and "x": add "es"
- ending in "y": change the "y" to "i" and add "es"
- ending in "f" or "fe": change the "f" or "fe" to "v" and add "es"
- ending in "o": add "s" or "es"

Some nouns stay the same in plural. Some nouns change in spelling.

C. Complete the crossword puzzle with the plural form of the clue words.

Across

A. family
B. cello
C. life
D. salmon
E. deer
F. potato

Down

1. mouse
2. glass
3. peach
4. pond

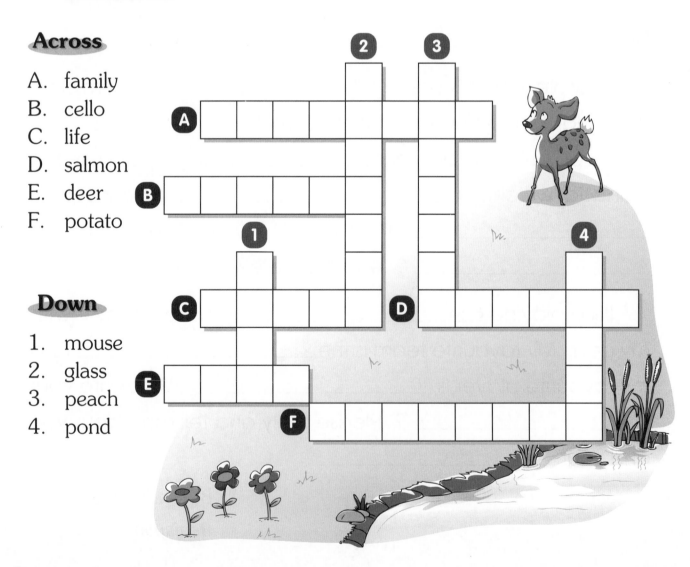

ISBN: 978-1-897457-03-0

Collective Nouns

A **collective noun** is a name for a group of people or things. It takes a singular or plural verb.

When the noun is considered as a single unit, a singular verb is used.

Example: The <u>team is</u> trying hard to win the game.

When the noun is seen as individuals, a plural verb is used.

Example: The <u>crew are</u> lining up at the gate.

D. Draw lines to match the collective nouns with the people they describe.

1. class   ○

2. army   ○

3. team   ○

4. crew   ○

5. family   ○

○ **A** workers

○ **B** parents and the children

○ **C** students

○ **D** soldiers

○ **E** players

E. Circle the correct words to complete the sentences.

1. The team is / are doing its best to prepare for the playoff.

2. On the last day of school, the class have / has to clear their lockers.

3. Her family plan / plans to go to Brazil at Easter.

4. The orchestra was / were voted the best in Toronto last year.

5. The army is / are sent to the country for peacekeeping.

unit 2 Pronouns and Possessives

Pronouns

A **pronoun** replaces a noun. It can be the subject or object of a sentence.

Subject pronouns: I, you, we, they, he, she, it

Object pronouns: me, you, us, them, him, her, it

Example: Anita has a parrot. <u>She</u> talks to <u>it</u> every day.

"She" replaces "Anita"; "it" replaces "parrot".

A. Draw lines to match the nouns with the subject pronouns.

1. The dolphin

2. Mom

3. Joe and Calvin

4. Dad and I

5. Mr. Downey

He

She

It

We

They

B. Write the object pronouns for the nouns.

1. my brother and me   _____

2. the door   _____

3. Jeff   _____

4. the teapot and the cups   _____

5. my grandmother   _____

ISBN: 978-1-897457-03-0

C. Check ✔ if the underlined pronouns are correct. If not, write the correct ones on the lines.

1. The Easter eggs are beautiful. I will take <u>it</u> home. _____

2. Mary likes reading comics. <u>He</u> finishes one comic book in one day. _____

3. They could not get on the bus because <u>it</u> was too crowded. _____

4. My father bought <u>I</u> a big gift. _____

5. Danny and I went to the beach. <u>We</u> had a lot of fun. _____

D. Fill in the blanks with appropriate pronouns.

Dad took us to Niagara Falls last Saturday because Grandpa came to visit us from Vancouver.

Mom and Dad got up early because 1._____ had to prepare for the trip. I woke up early to help 2._____ too. It took 3._____ about an hour to get there. 4._____ arrived there at about ten o'clock. Grandpa was very excited to see the Falls. 5._____ kept asking us to take pictures for him. "Will 6._____ send 7._____ the photos, my grandson?" he asked. "Of course," 8._____ said.

Mom made some sandwiches for lunch. 9._____ brought some fruit too. After lunch, we went to the Imax Theatre and saw a movie about daredevils.

Possessive Adjectives

A **possessive adjective** describes a noun that follows it. It tells who possesses or is related to the noun.

Possessive adjectives: my, your, our, their, his, her, its

Example: Shawn and <u>his</u> brother clean <u>their</u> room once a week.

E.   Circle the correct words to complete the sentences.

1.   Barry hit a home run; it was his / her biggest hit in the game.

2.   I had me / my hair cut last week.

3.   Amy left hers / her diary in the library.

4.   The cat is looking for it / its mother.

5.   Have you finished your / its homework?

6.   Look at that dress. I like my / its pattern.

7.   Sandy plays with her / she puppy every day.

8.   We should wash my / our hands before meals.

9.   The children made our / their wishes in front of the pond.

10.   Mr. Tee always comes to his / our house when we are having dinner.

11.   Mr. and Mrs. McArthur are looking forward to them / their wedding anniversary.

ISBN: 978-1-897457-03-0

Possessive Pronouns

A **possessive pronoun** tells who possesses something or is related to someone.

Possessive pronouns: mine, yours, ours, theirs, his, hers

Example: David gave his roller skates to me. They are <u>mine</u> now.

"Mine" refers to my roller skates. It is not followed by a noun.

F.   Rewrite the sentences using possessive pronouns.

Example: *This is your teddy bear.*
             This teddy bear is yours.

1.   This is my bracelet.

    _____

2.   This is our tree house.

    _____

3.   That is Uncle Tim's guitar.

    _____

4.   Those are Jerry and Daisy's pictures.

    _____

5.   These are Judy's shoes.

    _____

6.   Those are your rackets.

    _____

ISBN: 978-1-897457-03-0

unit 3 Verbs

Past Tense Verbs

A **past tense verb** tells what happened at a past time. Most past tense verbs are formed by adding "d" or "ed" to the base form.

Examples: smile → smiled   pick → picked

Some past tense verbs are irregular.

Examples: do → did   break → broke

Other past tense verbs are the same as the base form.

Examples: cut → cut   shed → shed

A. Complete the crossword puzzle with the past form of the clue words.

Across

A. bet
B. forget
C. drink
D. make
E. watch

Down

1. fear
2. shake
3. buy
4. become

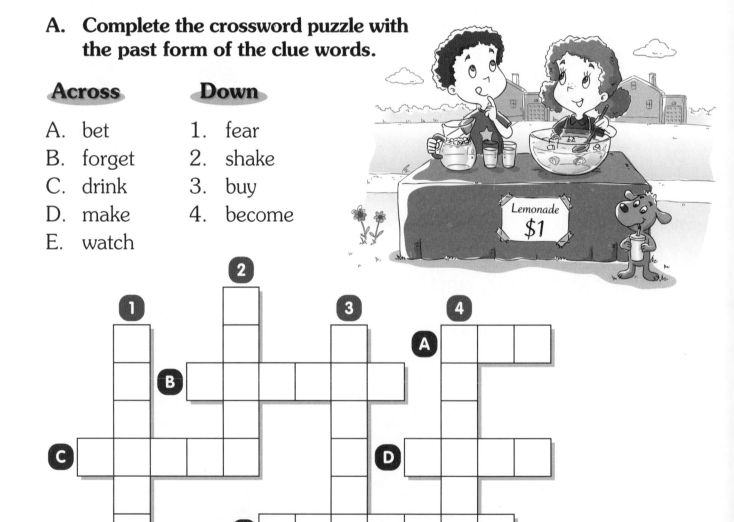

B. Circle the correct past tense verbs to complete the sentences.

For most verbs ending in "y", change the "y" to "i" before adding "ed".

1. The hen layed / laid some eggs this morning.

2. I read / readed the news last night.

3. My sister found / founded her glasses.

4. A golf ball hit / hitted the window of their house.

5. Ken and Gary studyed / studied for the quiz.

C. Complete the story with the past form of the words.

go   throw   bring
jump   take   catch
be   play   help

Mr. and Mrs. Jones 1._____ for a holiday last week.

We 2._____ them look after their dog Billy.   I

3._____ him out to the park and 4._____ with

him. I 5._____ a ball with me. Billy 6._____ so

excited to see it. When I 7._____ the ball over him, he

8._____ high and 9._____ it.

Verbs with Modals

Modals are words that help verbs. Sometimes, they change the meaning of the sentences. The base form of verbs is used after most modals. **"Can"** is used to show ability or permission.

Examples: I <u>can</u> make a pyramid with these cards.
You <u>can</u> go now.

"Should" is used to show obligation or advice.

Examples: We <u>should</u> wear seat belts in cars.
You <u>should</u> give it a try.

D. Circle the correct words in the following sentences.

1. You can / should borrow my bike.

2. Bob can / should say "sorry" to you.

3. We can / should listen to our parents.

4. Bridget can / should solve the puzzle.

5. You can / should knock at the door before you go in.

6. Can / Should I set the alarm clock at six o'clock?

7. The audience can / should see the performer clearly.

8. They can / should clean up the mess.

9. You can / should have cake or ice cream for dessert.

10. Do you think they can / should win?

ISBN: 978-1-897457-03-0

E. Fill in the blanks with "can" or "should" and the words on the door.

reach
give
help
take
pay
scare

1. Our little dog _____ strangers away.

2. Samantha _____ the candies on the shelf.

3. They _____ each other at school.

4. We _____ attention in class.

5. Don't worry. Dad _____ you a ride.

6. You _____ my umbrella. I don't need it.

F. Put the words in order to form sentences.

1. open   books   the   now   you   can

   _____

2. David   build   blocks   house   the   a   with   can

   _____

3. not   they   me   names   call   should

   _____

   _____

4. here   left   we   turn   should

   _____

   _____

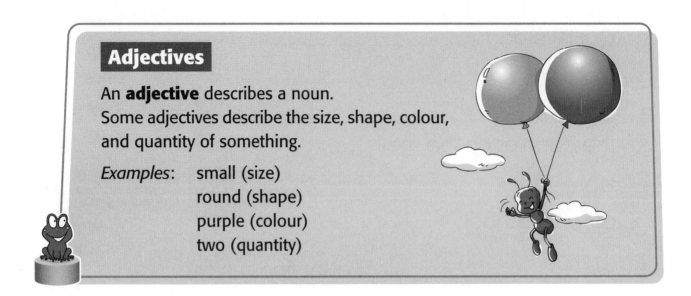

unit 4 Adjectives and Adverbs

Adjectives

An **adjective** describes a noun.
Some adjectives describe the size, shape, colour, and quantity of something.

Examples: small (size)
round (shape)
purple (colour)
two (quantity)

A.   Read the clues. Fill in the missing letters to form the correct adjectives.

1.   the shape of the Canadian flag   __ __c__ __ __g__ __ar

2.   the biggest single digit number   __i__e

3.   very big   __ __g__

4.   very small   __ __ __y

5.   the colour of snow   __h__ __ e

6.   a dozen   __ __ __ __ve

B.   Draw the following objects in the spaces provided.

1.   one big yellow square clock

2.   three long blue sticks

ISBN: 978-1-897457-03-0

Some adjectives describe how something looks, sounds, smells, etc. or how you feel about it.

Examples: pretty (look)
noisy (sound)
sweet (smell)
comfortable (feeling)

C. Draw lines to match the adjectives with the nouns they describe.

1. difficult •

2. young •

3. colourful •

4. strong •

5. stormy •

6. exciting •

• fence

• game

• woman

• weather

• umbrella

• examination

D. Fill in the blanks with the suitable adjectives.

fierce   crowded   amazing   useful   upset   sour

1. The show was _____ . We all enjoyed it.

2. The lemon is really _____ . I need to add more sugar to the iced tea.

3. Vicky is very _____ because she is going to move.

4. This bus is too _____ . Let's wait for the next one.

5. Take the compass with you; it's _____ .

6. The lion looks _____ and we dare not get close to it.

Comparative Adjectives

A **comparative adjective** compares two nouns.
For adjectives with one syllable, add "er" to form the comparative.

Example: My hair is <u>longer</u> than yours.

For adjectives with two or more syllables, add "more".

Example: This quiz is <u>more difficult</u> than the last one.

For adjectives ending in "y", change the "y" to "i" before adding "er".

Example: Fruits are <u>healthier</u> than chocolates.

E.   Complete the chart with the correct adjectives.

Original	Comparative		Original	Comparative
1. useful			2. strong	
3.	easier		4.	more spacious
5. lucky			6.	deeper

F.   Fill in the blanks with the comparative form of the adjectives.

1.   My Christmas gift seems (heavy) _____ than yours.

2.   Chocolate is (tasty) _____ than gum.

3.   It's (dark) _____ in the room than outside.

4.   The new roller coaster is (exciting) _____ than the haunted house.

ISBN: 978-1-897457-03-0

Adverbs

An **adverb** describes a verb. It tells how an action takes place. Most adverbs are formed by adding "ly" to the adjectives.

Example: Mom is making a timetable <u>carefully</u>.

Others are irregular.

Examples: I am studying <u>hard</u> for the quiz.
We'll <u>probably</u> go to the cottage.
The boy looked at the toys <u>greedily</u>.

G. Fill in the blanks with the adverbs of the given words.

1. How (far) _____ do we have to fly?

2. The woman was (extreme) _____ thrilled when she saw her son.

3. Whenever I see this pose, I (natural) _____ think of Tina.

4. This Halloween costume fits you (good) _____ .

5. I was so tired that I fell asleep (quick) _____ .

6. Donna sang (sweet) _____ on the stage.

7. Mom spread the cream (even) _____ on the cake.

8. Mark swims very (fast) _____ . I can't catch up with him.

9. Their grandparents are looking at them (happy) 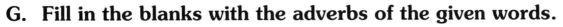 _____ .

Prepositions

Some **prepositions** tell where someone or something is: in, on, in front of, behind, beside, over, above, under, on top of.

Example: There are some Easter eggs <u>in</u> the basket.

A. Look at the pictures. Circle the correct prepositions.

1. Place a book [in / on] the balloon.

2. There is a snowman [in front of / behind] the house.

3. There is a fish [in / on] the bowl.

4. The man is holding a trophy [over / under] his head.

5. Tom is sitting [behind / beside] Mary.

ISBN: 978-1-897457-03-0

B. **Look at the picture and read the sentences. Check ✔ if the underlined preposition in each sentence is correct. If not, write the correct one on the line.**

1. Carl is sitting <u>on</u> the sofa. _____

2. Kylie the Chameleon is <u>over</u> the sofa too. _____

3. The cats are playing <u>behind</u> the sofa. _____

4. There is a plant <u>beside</u> the sofa. _____

5. There is a lamp <u>on top of</u> the sofa. _____

6. There is a letter <u>on</u> the table. _____

7. There is a mirror <u>in</u> the wall. _____

C. **Draw the following in the picture in (B).**

- a pen under the table
- a butterfly above the plant
- a clock beside the mirror

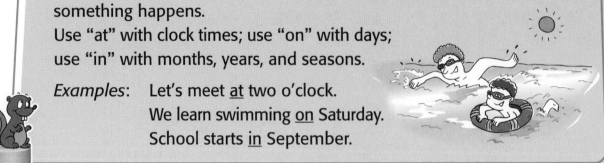

Some prepositions tell when someone does something or when something happens.
Use "at" with clock times; use "on" with days;
use "in" with months, years, and seasons.

Examples: Let's meet <u>at</u> two o'clock.
We learn swimming <u>on</u> Saturday.
School starts <u>in</u> September.

D. Draw lines to match the prepositions with the times.

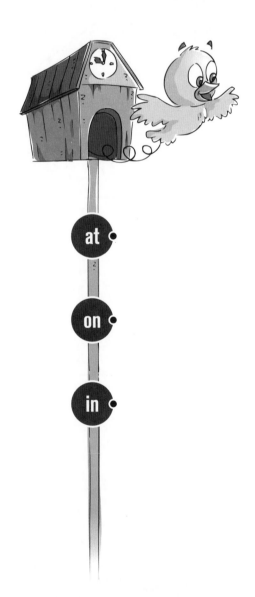

- 1998

- Boxing Day

- winter

- the last day of 2009

- half past six

- June

- Monday

- eight twenty-two

- the year she was born

- Mother's Day

- My first day in Halifax

- February

ISBN: 978-1-897457-03-0

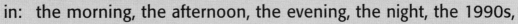

Note the following uses:
at: dawn, sunrise, noon, dusk, sunset, night, midnight
on: Monday morning, 26th May, 2008
in: the morning, the afternoon, the evening, the night, the 1990s, the 20th century

E. Fill in the blanks with the correct prepositions.

1. We usually go grocery shopping _____ Saturday afternoon.

2. Never walk alone on the street late _____ the night.

3. What costume will you wear _____ Halloween?

4. This castle was built _____ the 1870s.

5. We meet _____ the last Sunday of every month.

6. The scenery here is splendid, especially _____ sunset.

7. I'll give you a call _____ the evening.

8. My baby brother was born _____ 3rd July, 2007.

9. That bell chimes _____ three o'clock sharp every day.

10. They gathered for the countdown _____ New Year's Eve.

11. The movie starts _____ nine thirty _____ night.

12. The blackout took place _____ the hottest day _____ summer.

And, Or, and But

A conjunction joins words, phrases, or sentences together.
"And", **"or"**, and **"but"** are some of the common conjunctions.

Examples: My parents <u>and</u> I will go to the zoo this weekend.
We will go on Saturday <u>or</u> Sunday.
My sister wants to go too, <u>but</u> she has to study for her test.

A. Circle the correct conjunctions.

1. Would you like to have banana pancake
and / or apple pie for dessert?

2. He likes soccer and / but he doesn't
like basketball.

3. You must hurry or / but you'll miss the bus.

4. I'll be busy on Sunday and / or Monday.
Can we go on Tuesday?

**B. Check ✔ if the underlined conjunctions are correct. If not, write
the correct ones on the lines.**

1. I can buy two gifts so I'll get the kaleidoscope
<u>and</u> the puzzle.   _____

2. Danny will come <u>or</u> Sandra won't.   _____

3. The doll is beautiful <u>or</u> it is expensive.   _____

4. Did Team A <u>or</u> Team B win the game?   _____

5. Both Jenny <u>or</u> Clara are my best friends.   _____

ISBN: 978-1-897457-03-0

C. Match the sentences on the left with the related ones on the right. Write the letters.

1. He was sick. _____

2. The show was fabulous. _____

3. Don't forget the password. _____

4. We may stay at home tonight. _____

5. They love pets. _____

A He did not see the doctor.

B They have four cats.

C We all enjoyed it very much.

D We will go to the cinema.

E You can't log on the computer.

D. Join the related sentences in (C) with "and", "or", or "but".

1. _____

_____

2. _____

_____

3. _____

_____

4. _____

_____

5. _____

_____

Because and So

"**Because**" and "**so**" are two other common conjunctions.
"Because" is used to give a reason.

Example: Tina is angry <u>because</u> James called her names.

"So" is used to tell a result.

Example: I could jump over you <u>so</u> I won.

E.   Fill in the blanks with "because" or "so".

1. Mom went to visit Grandma _____ I helped out at home.

2. The whirlpool was crowded _____ I went to the diving pool.

3. I like Olivia very much _____ she is kind and helpful.

4. Her scale was broken _____ she is buying a new one.

5. Susan is crying _____ she misses her poodle.

6. The birds migrate to the south _____ it is very cold here in winter.

7. The dessert tastes better when it is cold _____ Mom put it in the fridge last night.

8. He tossed away the popcorn _____ it was stale.

9. Kate helped me with my homework _____ I am making her a thank-you card.

ISBN: 978-1-897457-03-0

F. Complete the following sentences by circling the correct words and write the letters on the lines.

A	we're going to the beach
B	we went to an Indian restaurant
C	you have to teach me
D	he did well in the quiz
E	we need to return these books

1. I've never flown a kite before because / so _____ .

2. We're packing some snacks and drinks because / so _____ .

3. Ken got a gift because / so _____ .

4. Auntie Betty likes curry because / so _____ .

5. Today is the due date because / so _____ .

G. Complete the following sentences with your own words.

1. Charles did not go to school today because _____

_____ .

2. Uncle Tim bought a new digital camera so _____

_____ .

3. _____

because she forgot to hand in her homework.

4. _____

so I stayed inside all day.

A. Read the story. Circle all the proper nouns.

Tim is a droplet of water. He lives with many other

droplets of water in a very small and crowded place. He doesn't know how

he got stuck there. All that he can remember is one day he opened his eyes

and found himself there.

Tim likes looking up at an <u>opening</u> above them – in fact, it's the only thing

that looks different from the boring surroundings. He can always see a <u>patch</u>

of yellow. Sometimes new droplets come rushing in from there. He asks

every new <u>member</u> what is out there beyond the opening, but everyone is as

ignorant as he is. Still, Tim is sure that there is something else outside.

Sometimes, droplets of water disappear as suddenly as others appear.

There have been <u>rumours</u> about the disappearances:

Polly says, "There are yellow <u>elves</u> outside. Our friends must have

been kidnapped by them!"

"No, it's a wicked <u>fairy</u> in a yellow <u>cape</u>. She uses our friends in her magic

<u>potion</u>!" Leon says.

Jack exclaims, "They've been sucked into that yellow nothingness!"

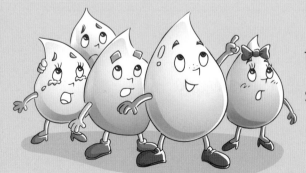

All droplets conclude, "No matter what

that thing is, it's dangerous! We should all

stay away from it."

But is it really dangerous? Tim wonders.

ISBN: 978-1-897457-03-0

B. Look at (A) again. Write the singular and plural forms of the underlined common nouns.

Singular Noun

Plural Noun

1. _____   _____
2. _____   _____
3. _____   _____
4. _____   _____
5. _____   _____
6. _____   _____
7. _____   _____
8. _____   _____

C. Circle the correct words to complete the paragraphs.

Tim wants to leave this boring home of 1. yours / his . He tells others 2. his / her idea. 3. We / They all think that 4. she / he is crazy.

" 5. It / They is really dangerous outside. 6. I / You shouldn't take the risk," Nina tells 7. him / me .

"Yes, 8. he / I agree with what 9. they / she says. You'd better stay here with 10. us / you ," Leon adds.

ISBN: 978-1-897457-03-0

D. Rewrite the following sentences by changing the underlined verbs into the past form.

1. Tim still <u>wants</u> to leave.

   _____

2. He <u>thinks</u> the world outside must be very exciting.

   _____

3. His friends <u>try</u> to persuade him to stay.

   _____

4. They <u>give</u> him advice on how to make life more interesting.

   _____

   _____

E. Complete what Tim's friends say with the correct modals.

We 1._____ play with you every day.
       can / should

I 2._____ tell you stories when you are bored.
     can / should

Never think about leaving. You 3._____ stay
                                    can / should
with us.

You 4._____ be happy to have friends like us.
       can / should

ISBN: 978-1-897457-03-0

F. Fill in the blanks with the correct form of the given adjectives or change them to adverbs.

Tim's desire of leaving is getting (strong) 1._____ with each passing day. Every day, he stares at the (yellow) 2._____ opening over him, thinking how he can get (close) 3._____ to it so he can jump out.

Then one day, something (special) 4._____ happens. A (long) 5._____ and green thing comes in from the opening. Then many more (new) 6._____ droplets join them. Tim has never found himself that close to the opening before. He is (real) 7._____ excited. He may be able to leave!

Tim bids farewell to his friends. They are all very (sad) 8._____ about his leaving. Jack is really (upset) 9._____ . He doesn't want his best friend to leave. He tries (desperate) 10._____ to persuade Tim to stay, but Tim's mind of leaving is set. With his greatest effort, Tim leaps from his friends and out through the opening he goes!

G. Check ✔ if the underlined preposition in each sentence is correct. If not, write the correct one on the line.

1. Tim jumps from his home <u>in</u> sunrise.

_____

2. He finds himself landing <u>at</u> a smooth surface.

_____

3. It is the surface of a cupboard <u>by</u> the window.   _____

4. He looks at the thing he has called home <u>beside</u> him. It's in fact a vase <u>in</u> the cupboard.   _____

   _____

5. He knows that his friends are still <u>under</u> there.   _____

6. The yellow patch <u>over</u> him has become much larger now. It is actually the ceiling of a room.   _____

7. A clock <u>in front of</u> the wall shows that it is six o'clock in the morning.   _____

   _____

8. The first ray of the sun shines <u>on</u> Tim. He feels warm and comfortable.   _____

9. Then Tim feels a very pleasant sensation <u>in</u> himself – he is becoming lighter and lighter.   _____

ISBN: 978-1-897457-03-0

H. Join each pair of sentences using the correct conjunction.

and   or   but   because   so

1. Tim finds himself becoming lighter and lighter. He is rising into the air.

    _____

    _____

2. He lets out a cry. He doesn't know what is going on.

    _____

    _____

3. His friends hear his cry. They ask him what is happening.

    _____

    _____

4. Tim can hear the voices of his friends. He can no longer answer them.

    _____

    _____

5. Is Tim dying? Is it the beginning of a new life for him?

    _____

    _____

ISBN: 978-1-897457-03-0

unit 7 Parts of a Sentence

A. **Underline the subjects in the following sentences.**

1. Ken held a birthday party last Sunday.

2. I went to his party with my sister.

3. We played lots of games.

4. We made some nice looking hats.

5. Billy has a small head.

6. His hat was too big for him.

7. The party finished at five o'clock.

B. **Match the subjects with the predicates. Write the letters.**

1. My cat   ____

2. The museum   ____

3. The weather   ____

4. His father   ____

5. Jennifer   ____

A is not suitable for an outing.

B gave birth to three kittens.

C is a famous actress.

D is near the subway station.

E is doing gardening in the backyard.

ISBN: 978-1-897457-03-0

Predicates

The **predicate** of a sentence is the part that describes the subject.

Example: Kitty <u>is making a cake</u>.

"Is making a cake" describes what Kitty is doing.

C.   In each sentence, put a vertical line between the subject and its predicate.

1.   The Royal Ontario Museum attracts a lot of visitors every year.

2.   The puppy and its mother are playing on the lawn.

3.   We brought our own lunch for the farm visit.

4.   This campaign aims at helping the homeless.

5.   The heavy rain caused floods in some areas.

6.   Ice hockey is very popular in Canada.

D.   Complete the sentences with suitable predicates.

1.   Thanksgiving Day _____

_____ .

2.   My school _____

_____ .

3.   Polar bears _____

_____ .

4.   Robin _____

_____ .

Subject-Verb Agreement

The verb that begins the predicate must agree with the subject.
If the subject is singular, a singular verb should be used.

Example: Sam <u>is</u> a firefighter.

If the subject is plural, a plural verb should be used.

Example: The <u>students</u> <u>like</u> their new teacher very much.

E.   Fill in the blanks with the correct verbs.

The sky (is / are) 1._____ blue.

The cow (go / goes) 2._____ moo.

The grass (is / are) 3._____ green.

We (eat / eats) 4._____ ice cream.

The clouds (is / are) 5._____ white.

We (fly / flies) 6._____ our kite.

The flowers (is / are) 7._____ red.

I (want / wants) 8._____ my bed.

ISBN: 978-1-897457-03-0

F. Circle the correct answers.

Mom and I 1. **love / loves** candies. Toffee 2. **is / are** her favourite. I 3. **like / likes** strawberry flavour best. We always 4. **have / has** candies when we 5. **is / are** watching television. Whenever Mom 6. **go / goes** shopping, she 7. **buy / buys** some candies. Dad 8. **don't / doesn't** like candies. He 9. **keep / keeps** reminding us to brush our teeth after eating candies and we always 10. **do / does** .

G. Check ✔ if the underlined words are correct. If not, write the correct ones on the lines.

1. The boys <u>is</u> singing in the music room. _____

2. Don't worry. My dog <u>don't</u> bite. _____

3. Everyone <u>leave</u> the classroom at recess. _____

4. There <u>is</u> only a few biscuits left. _____

5. Janet and Jason <u>belongs</u> to the tennis team. _____

6. My uncle <u>is</u> an actor. _____

7. Taking photos <u>isn't</u> too difficult. _____

8. <u>Are</u> your mom a yoga instructor? _____

unit 8 Types of Sentences

Telling Sentences and Asking Sentences

A **telling sentence** tells something. It ends with a period (.).

Examples: Janet doesn't like hiking.
              She likes cycling instead.

An **asking sentence** asks about something. It ends with a question mark (?).

Examples: Are you coming with me?
              Or do you want to stay here?

A. Read the sentences. Add a period for a telling sentence. Add a question mark for an asking sentence.

1. There are no more eggs in the fridge

2. Mr. Weir's car is in the driveway

3. Can we have some snacks before the show

4. No one knows what is going on

5. Are they coming for the party

6. How do we go to the library from here

7. We can watch a video tonight

8. This book is not mine

9. Did he draw it on his own

10. Do you think he can make it

ISBN: 978-1-897457-03-0

B. Put the words in order to make telling sentences.

1. the   her   in   room   teacher   is

   _____

2. have   you   can   a   piece

   _____

3. told   interesting   Mom   last   me   an   story   night

   _____

4. a   there   around   restaurant   is   corner   new   the

   _____

   _____

   _____

C. Read the telling sentences below and make asking sentences.

1. The catcher is Jason's brother.

   Who _____

2. The Red Team is winning.

   Which _____

3. Don is on third base.

   Where _____

4. Baseball is our favourite sport.

   What _____

5. We will play again tomorrow afternoon.

   When _____

Imperative Sentences and Exclamatory Sentences

An **imperative sentence** tells someone to do or not to do something. It ends with a period (.).

Examples: Don't leave the lights on.
                Turn them off when you leave the room.

An **exclamatory sentence** shows strong feelings like sudden surprise, excitement, or pain. It ends with an exclamation mark (!).

Examples: What a fabulous magic show!
                That's really amazing!

D.   Check ✔ if the sentences end with the correct punctuation marks. If not, put the correct ones in the boxes.

1.   Oops, I dropped the vase. ☐

2.   Wow, that's awesome! ☐

3.   Draw a bird in the nest. ☐

4.   Ouch, it really hurts. ☐

5.   Please pass me the salt and pepper! ☐

6.   What a wonderful girl she is. ☐

7.   How ridiculous! ☐

8.   Let's meet at the theatre! ☐

9.   Yuck, it's gone stale. ☐

10. Do not feed the geese. ☐

ISBN: 978-1-897457-03-0

E. Look at the pictures. Write an imperative sentence or an exclamatory sentence to tell what each person is saying.

1. _____

2. _____

3. _____

4. _____

5. _____

6. _____

unit 9 Tenses

A. Fill in the blanks with the correct form of the given words.

enjoy   be   walk   meet   play   drive   have   learn
teach   know   be   work   be   buy   like   go

Mrs. Williams 1._____ our neighbour. She 2._____ two pet dogs. She 3._____ them every evening. I sometimes 4._____ with her and 5._____ with her dogs. Mrs. Williams 6._____ her dogs simple tricks and they 7._____ fast. They 8._____ really clever.

Mrs. Williams 9._____ in a farmer's market. She 10._____ to work every day. The fruits and vegetables 11._____ very fresh. Many people 12._____ produce there.

Mrs. Williams 13._____ talking with everyone she 14._____ . People also 15._____ talking with her because she 16._____ a lot about fruits and vegetables.

ISBN: 978-1-897457-03-0

The negative of the simple present tense is formed by adding "do not" or "does not" before the base form of the verb. For the verb "be", use "is/am/are not".

"Do not" is used with plural subjects, "you", and "I".
"Does not" is used with third person singular subjects.

Examples: The leaves of this tree <u>do not fall</u> in winter.
My father <u>does not drink</u> beer.
I <u>am not</u> Tim.

B. Change the sentences into negative.

1. These roses smell sweet.

_____

2. Badminton is popular in our school.

_____

3. Grace has a new skateboard.

_____

4. They go to their cottage every summer.

_____

5. There are many people in the restaurant.

_____

6. I am hungry.

_____

7. Laura wants to learn swimming.

_____

Simple Past Tense

The **simple past tense** is used to tell past actions.

The negative of the simple past tense is formed by adding "did not" before the base form of the verb.
For the verb "be", use "was/were not".

Examples: Nancy <u>fell</u> off the bike yesterday.
Charles <u>did not understand</u> the problem.
We <u>were not</u> neighbours.

C. Fill in the blanks with the correct form of the given words.

1. My dog (drink) _____ milk when it was little.

2. The pizza we had (not be) _____ tasty.

3. May (go) _____ cherry-picking last weekend.

4. We (not wear) _____ uniforms in our high school.

5. They (meet) _____ in Hawaii two years ago.

D. Change these sentences into negative.

1. We rested under the tree.

   _____

2. It was hot.

   _____

3. We had ice cream.

   _____

4. Paul and I were classmates.

   _____

ISBN: 978-1-897457-03-0

Simple Future Tense

The **simple future tense** is used to tell future actions.

Add "will" before the base form of the verb to form the simple future tense.

Examples: I <u>will see</u> you tonight.
            She <u>will give</u> you a call.

The negative of the simple future tense is formed by adding "will not" or "won't" before the base form of the verb.

Examples: I <u>won't forget</u> you.
            He <u>will not run</u> away.

E. Complete the answers.

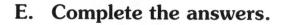

1. Will you jump on me?

   No, I _____ you.

2. Will Roger feed the cat?

   Yes, _____ the cat.

3. Will it rain this afternoon?

   No, _____ this afternoon.

4. Will they go to the lake this weekend?

   No, _____ this weekend.

5. Will Dad come home for dinner?

   Yes, _____ for dinner.

6. Will the centre be closed next Sunday?

   Yes, _____ next Sunday.

unit 10 Forming Questions

Yes/No Questions

A **yes/no question** expects a yes or no answer.

A yes/no question often begins with "Do/Does/Did" or a modal like "Can/May", followed by the subject and the base form of the verb.

Examples: Do you practise often?
Can you turn a somersault?

A. Check ✔ the correct questions. Cross ✘ the wrong ones.

1. _____ Do you want some candies?

2. _____ Must we take the earliest bus?

3. _____ Does she speaks French?

4. _____ Did they tell you the result?

5. _____ Do eat they spicy food?

B. Put the words in order to form questions. Use capitals and question marks.

1. in   time   they   could   finish   project   their

_____

2. your   beef   does   cat   eat

_____

3. the   rules   the   did   zookeeper   tell   her

_____

4. computer   do   you   your   room   have   a   in

_____

ISBN: 978-1-897457-03-0

Sometimes, a yes/no question begins with "Is/Am/Are/Was/Were", followed by the subject.

Examples: Is that yours?
Am I the one to do it?
Were you surprised to see Gordon?

C. Circle the correct words to complete the questions.

1. Are / Do they tired after the long walk?

2. Am / Is I going with you?

3. Is / Does Alison the oldest child?

4. Was / Were they in the drama club last year?

5. Is / Does skiing a popular sport in your country?

D. Complete the following questions with your own words.

1. Are the lollipops _____ _____ ?

2. Am I _____ _____ ?

3. Are you _____ _____ ?

4. Was he _____ ?

5. Were they _____ ?

Question Words

We use **question words** to ask for information. For example, to find out about a concert, we can ask the following:

who – the performers
what – the program
when – date and time
where – location
why – purpose

Example: Who will be singing at the concert?

E. Circle the correct words to complete the questions.

1. What / Why is wrong with him?

2. Who / Where did you put my book?

3. Who / When gave you the necklace?

4. Why / What did he do to the plant?

5. Why / How are you mad at her?

6. Who / How did you make this dessert?

7. When / Where is Jason?

8. Who / When will you go fishing?

9. Why / What is she crying?

ISBN: 978-1-897457-03-0

F. Match the questions with the answers. Write the letters.

1. Who told you that? _____

2. Where did you see Anita? _____

3. Why do you need to buy a new racket? _____

4. What did you add to the chicken curry? _____

5. When did your parents get married? _____

6. How could you make this bookmark? _____

Ⓐ In the library
Ⓑ Peter
Ⓒ I asked Dad to help me.
Ⓓ Because mine is broken
Ⓔ In 1990
Ⓕ A teaspoon of coffee

G. Read the answers. Complete the questions.

1. Why _____ ?

   Ryan stayed at home because he was sick.

2. When _____ ?

   I took this picture two years ago.

3. How _____ ?

   I can remove the seat by pulling the red handle.

4. What _____ ?

   I am reading a comic book.

unit 11 Contractions and Abbreviations

Contractions

A **contraction** is a short way of writing two words. One or more letters are taken out and replaced with an apostrophe.

Examples: do not → don't
we have → we've
she is → she's

A. Draw lines to match the words with their contractions.

1.	what is	
2.	I will	
3.	they are	
4.	he has	
5.	should not	
6.	you have	

shouldn't
you've
what's
he's
I'll
they're

B. Circle the correct words to complete the sentences.

1. Wow! It's / Its freezing.

2. They wern't / weren't at home when I called.

3. She wiln't / won't give in.

4. I don't / donn't agree with you.

5. We havn't / haven't had lunch yet.

ISBN: 978-1-897457-03-0

C. Fill in the blanks with contractions for the given words.

1. Sorry, (I am) _____ afraid I (cannot) _____ go.

2. We (must not) _____ forget our way out the woods.

3. Fiona is busy. (She is) _____ doing her Math project.

4. (We are) _____ going to be there soon.

5. Josh (does not) _____ like spicy food.

6. (They have) _____ gone fishing.

7. (He is) _____ pulling the rope.

D. Rewrite the sentences using contractions.

1. He has been to Italy before.

   _____

2. She will call us when she arrives.

   _____

3. They could not find the restaurant.

   _____

4. We did not watch the game last night.

   _____

   _____

5. I would rather stay at home.

   _____

   _____

ISBN: 978-1-897457-03-0

Abbreviations

An **abbreviation** is the shortened form of a word or words.

Examples: January → Jan.
Mister → Mr.
centimetre → cm
National Hockey League → NHL

E. Check ✔ if the underlined word in each sentence is an abbreviation.

1. Her birthday is on <u>Dec.</u>12.   _____

2. You <u>don't</u> understand what I mean.   _____

3. <u>Mrs.</u> Ronsdat is our class teacher.   _____

4. <u>Let's</u> meet at the mall entrance.   _____

5. The game starts at 3:00 <u>p.m.</u> today.   _____

F. Draw lines to match the abbreviations with their standard form.

1. Dr.	February
2. Blvd.	Boulevard
3. vs.	before noon
4. km	Doctor
5. Feb.	television
6. U.K.	versus
7. TV	United Kingdom
8. a.m.	kilometre

ISBN: 978-1-897457-03-0

G. Write the abbreviation for each of the following.

1. British Columbia _____

2. March _____

3. Junior _____

4. Saint _____

5. Road _____

6. kilogram _____

7. Mountain _____

H. Rewrite the sentences by changing the abbreviations to the standard form.

Although abbreviations are acceptable in some situations, we should avoid using them in most cases.

1. Xmas is coming soon.

   _____

2. Her birthday is in Aug.

   _____

3. The cinema is on Spring Ave.

   _____

4. We will be free on Fri. and Sat.

   _____

5. N.Y. is on the east coast of the U.S.

   _____

ISBN: 978-1-897457-03-0

> ### Root Words
>
> A **root word** is the basic word from which other words are derived.
>
> *Example:*   amuse (root word)
>   amusing (adjective)
>   amusement (noun)

A. Circle the root words for the given words.

1. facial
   - face
   - fact

2. clearance
   - clean
   - clear

3. disability
   - able
   - probability

4. unforgettable
   - get
   - forget

5. childish
   - child
   - dish

6. historical
   - story
   - history

B. Build new words from the following root words.

1. stick   _____ (adjective)

   _____ (noun)

2. silent   _____ (adverb)

   _____ (noun)

3. collect _____ (noun)

   _____ (noun)

ISBN: 978-1-897457-03-0

C. Write the root words for the given words.

1. accurately _____

2. growth _____

3. independent _____

4. flatten _____

5. building _____

6. dislike _____

7. container _____

8. unreal _____

D. Rewrite the sentences by changing the underlined root words to suitable new words.

1. A pair of gloves is <u>dispense</u> in winter here.

    _____

2. Mr. Riggs is a really <u>response</u> coach.

    _____

3. I am training my dog to be <u>obey</u>.

    _____

4. The <u>origin</u> ending was not that heartbreaking.

    _____

5. Wow! This pizza pocket is really <u>taste</u>.

    _____

    _____

6. Gary is stacking up the blocks <u>care</u>.

    _____

    _____

ISBN: 978-1-897457-03-0

Prefixes "Un" and "Re"

A **prefix** is a group of letters added to the beginning of a word that changes the meaning of the word.

The prefix "**un**" means "not" or "opposite of".

Example: lucky – unlucky.

The prefix "**re**" means "to do again".

Example: organize – reorganize

E.   Read the clues and complete the crossword puzzle with "un" and "re" words.

Across

A.   not wanted
B.   think again
C.   not clean

Down

1.   take again
2.   not able
3.   not lucky
4.   do again
5.   not willing

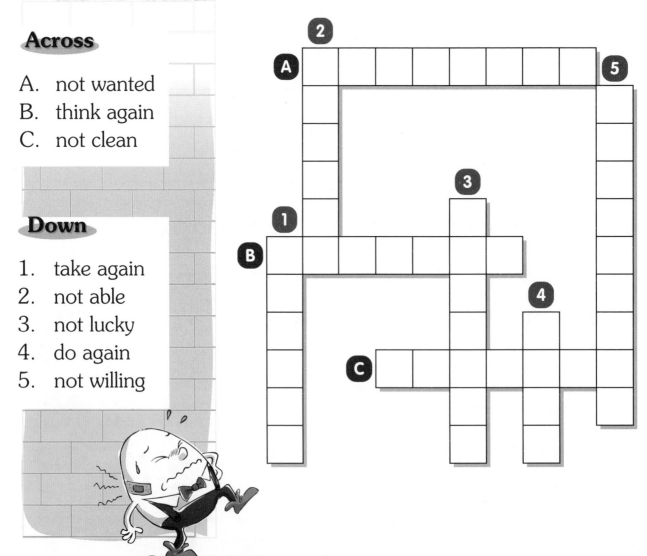

ISBN: 978-1-897457-03-0

F. Cross out ✗ the words where "un" or "re" is not a prefix.

university	regard
unlike	regain
undo	renew
under	rear
uncle	result
unknown	remake
unwind	restart
untouched	reopen
unite	reap

G. Rewrite the following sentences. Add "un" or "re" to the underlined words.

1. Natasha <u>told</u> the story in her own way.

   _____

2. The stepmother was <u>fair</u> to Natasha.

   _____

3. Natasha found the gate <u>locked</u>.

   _____

4. Natasha was finally able to <u>unite</u> with her sister.

   _____

Compound Words, Synonyms, Antonyms, and Homonyms

Compound Words

A **compound word** is formed when two words are put together to form a new word with a different meaning.

Example: fire + works = fireworks

A. Create as many compound words as you can with the words. Write the new words on the lines.

> Sometimes the same word can be used at the beginning of a compound word and sometimes it can be used at the end.

flower	house
book	work
store	light
sun	bed
shop	shoe
room	horse
worm	keeper

Welcome

_____

_____

_____

_____

_____

_____

_____

_____

ISBN: 978-1-897457-03-0

Synonyms

A **synonym** is a word that is similar in meaning to another word.

Example: pretty – beautiful

B. Complete the crossword puzzle with synonyms for the clue words.

Across

A. accomplish
B. differ
C. well-known
D. rapid

Down

1. crucial
2. named
3. fine
4. remain

> ### Antonyms
>
> An **antonym** is a word that is opposite in meaning to another word.
>
> *Example:*   big – small

C. Circle the antonyms for these words in the word search.

full	quiet	hot	hard
always	cheap	inside	near
weak	first	correct	appear

u	e	b	l	a	s	t	u	w	i	t	p	n	w	x	b	s
b	o	a	r	n	u	i	x	h	r	u	c	o	l	d	t	w
a	u	o	x	n	o	i	s	y	e	z	r	e	r	g	w	r
s	t	p	g	e	u	v	u	g	q	w	e	h	s	s	e	o
q	s	z	l	v	w	e	x	p	e	n	s	i	v	e	i	n
u	i	m	t	e	q	m	p	d	n	r	q	n	j	s	u	g
w	d	o	u	r	j	p	s	f	t	f	a	r	y	d	s	u
e	e	u	v	m	e	t	n	y	r	f	u	e	r	z	o	d
k	g	i	q	f	r	y	u	s	t	r	o	n	g	h	f	e
c	i	d	i	s	a	p	p	e	a	r	u	u	s	r	t	b

ISBN: 978-1-897457-03-0

Homonyms

A **homonym** is a word that sounds the same as another word, but has a different meaning and spelling.

Example: pale – pail

D. Fill in the blanks with homonyms of the given words.

> fare   tale   cell   root
>
> role   sweet   maid   genes   our

1. The kids do not want to _____ their toys in the garage sale.

2. Can I have another _____ to go with the soup?

3. Her new handbag is _____ of leather.

4. They will be here in an _____ .

5. Which _____ do you live in?

6. His dog has a long _____ .

7. That's not _____ ! How come he has two chocolate bars?

8. This is the shortest _____ to the park.

9. Oh! I love your _____ .

ISBN: 978-1-897457-03-0

A. Draw a vertical line to separate the subject and the predicate of each sentence.

1. Tim is rising into the air.

2. The faint voices of his friends are fading.

3. All his sensations are leaving him too.

4. He is no longer a water droplet.

5. There seems to be nothing left of him.

6. Everything comes to an absolute stillness.

B. Circle the correct words to complete the sentences. Pay attention to subject-verb agreement.

After what *1.* seem / seems like an instant, Tim *2.* is / are able to hear noises again. *3.* He / They opens his eyes and *4.* see / sees billions of water droplets crowded around him. They *5.* am / are all listening attentively to a really big droplet in the middle of the crowd.

"My dear fellows, *6.* I / we are here today to witness the formation of the Cloud Alliance. The day for the Great Jump *7.* is / are approaching. Let's celebrate!" the huge droplet *8.* say / says . All droplets *9.* respond / responds with thunderous applause.

ISBN: 978-1-897457-03-0

C. Put the words in order to form sentences. Add the proper punctuation at the end of the sentences. Then write what types of sentences they are. Use the letters below.

T – Telling Sentence
A – Asking Sentence
I – Imperative Sentence
E – Exclamatory Sentence

CLOUD ALLIANCE

Tim

1. Alliance to Cloud Welcome the

_____

2. the What Jump Great is

_____

3. It when to event we down an together Earth's is jump the surface

_____

_____

4. that Wow, exciting sounds

_____

5. ready for Let's Great the get Jump

_____

6. when hesitate jump Don't you

_____

ISBN: 978-1-897457-03-0

D. Rewrite each of the following sentences using the tense given.

1. Tim was happy to be a member of the Cloud Alliance.
   (Simple Present)

   _____

   _____

2. He does not want to leave his friends. (Simple Past)

   _____

   _____

3. But he also knows that he cannot stay in that cramped place
   with them. (Simple Past)

   _____

   _____

4. He made lots of new friends in the Alliance. (Simple Present)

   _____

   _____

5. He learned a lot from other members
   of the Alliance. (Simple Future)

   _____

   _____

   _____

6. The day for the Great Jump is
   coming soon. (Simple Future)

   _____

   _____

ISBN: 978-1-897457-03-0

E. Write Tim's questions.

Tim wants to know more about the Cloud Alliance and the Great Jump. He is talking to his new friend, Josh.

1. _____

   The name of that large droplet is Norman.

2. _____

   Yes, he is the leader of the Cloud Alliance.

3. _____

   The Great Jump is important because all living things on Earth need us.

4. _____

   We are going to land on mountains and in valleys, rivers, and oceans.

5. _____

   The Great Jump will take place when we have enough members in the Alliance.

6. _____

   Yes, you can jump with me.

ISBN: 978-1-897457-03-0

F. Write the contractions or abbreviations of the words in the blanks.

Tim and Josh are looking at people and things on Earth.

"Look at that mountain. It is 1._____ Mount 2._____

Everest. It is 3._____ 8848 metres 4._____ high. That

big country is Canada. It is 5._____ October 6._____

according to Earth's time, so the maple leaves have turned into

shades of red, orange, and yellow," Josh tells Tim.

"What is 7._____ that country south of Canada?" Tim

asks.

"That is 8._____ the United States 9._____," Josh

answers.

"See that old man walking in the park? I heard people call

him Mister 10._____ Oakman. He lives with his wife on East

Gate Avenue 11._____. Their son, Tom, visits them every

Thursday 12._____. Tom is a Royal Canadian Mounted Police

13._____ officer. They are 14._____ very proud of him."

While Josh is telling Tim about what he knows, there is

15._____ a sudden uproar among the members of the Cloud

Alliance.

"Let us 16._____ get over there to see what is

17._____ happening," Josh says.

ISBN: 978-1-897457-03-0

G. Fill in the blanks with the synonyms (S), antonyms (A), and homonyms (H) of the given words. Then follow Tim's instruction to complete the activity.

Norman, the 1._____ of the Cloud Alliance, is speaking
        leader (S)

2._____ to the crowd, "The time for the Great Jump has
    softly (A)

3._____ arrived. I know that 4._____ of you may
   eventually (S)   sum (H)

find it 5._____ to part with your 6._____ , but let me
         easy (A)   enemies (A)

assure you: we'll reunite 7._____ day! It's unwise to
                              won (H)

8._____ here. The living things on Earth 9._____ us.
   leave (A)   knead (H)

There's 10._____ that can replace us. So, let's not hesitate!"
          something (A)

On the count of three, all members jump. Tim has

11._____ felt this excited before. He is uncertain about where
    always (A)

he will land, but there is one thing he can tell for sure: leaving that

12._____ space he once got stuck in was a 13._____
    tiny (S)   correct (S)

decision. He has learned a lot 14._____ since then.
                                   less (A)

Circle the words with prefixes in the paragraphs above.

ISBN: 978-1-897457-03-0

We are cheery birds.

cheery

ISBN: 978-1-897457-03-0

1 Creatures of the Galapagos Islands

The Galapagos Islands are located approximately 950 kilometres off the coast of South America. These islands are famous for their <u>unique</u> vegetation and wildlife. Two of the unusual <u>creatures</u> found on these islands are the Galapagos Tortoise and the Marine Iguana.

The Galapagos Tortoise is the largest living tortoise. It has a huge shell made of bone. A male tortoise can grow to be over one metre long and can have a mass of over 200 kilograms. It can <u>effortlessly</u> carry a full-grown adult on its back. This slow-moving reptile has elephant-like feet with short toes. The Galapagos Tortoise is a <u>herbivore</u> that eats prickly pear cactus and fruits, water ferns, leaves, and grasses. During the day, this animal can <u>typically</u> be found <u>basking</u> in the hot sun or cooling itself in a lake or under a shady tree. A Galapagos Tortoise has another amazing <u>characteristic</u>. It can live to be 100 to 150 years old.

Another <u>extraordinary</u> animal found on the rocky shoreline of the Galapagos Islands is the Marine Iguana. This reptile is the only sea-going lizard in the world. It has razor-sharp teeth and long claws. It can grow to <u>approximately</u> one

metre in length. The Marine Iguana feeds on marine algae and seaweed found on either <u>exposed</u> rocks or in the cold seawater. The Marine Iguana spends much of its day lying in the sun warming its body and then diving into the ocean to find something to eat.

ISBN: 978-1-897457-03-0

A. Use the underlined words in the passage to complete the crossword puzzle.

Across

A. not exactly

B. uncovered, without protection

C. lying in warmth and sunshine

D. an animal that feeds mainly on plants

E. any living persons or animals

Down

1. having no like or equal

2. feature that makes something recognizable

3. involving little or no effort

4. representing a particular type of person or thing

5. different from others

B. Using the information found in the passage, complete the following Venn Diagram.

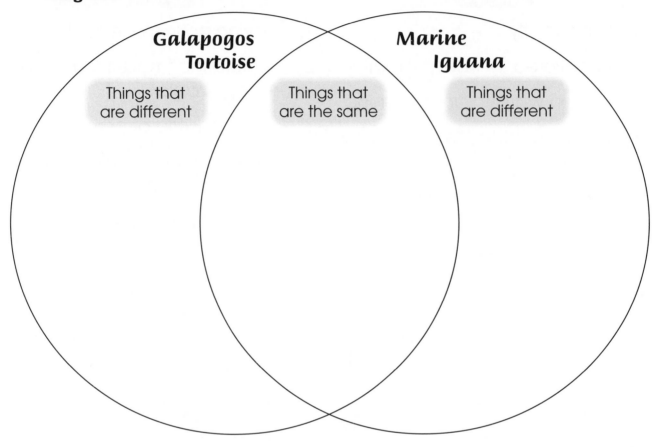

Galapogos Tortoise

Marine Iguana

Things that are different

Things that are the same

Things that are different

C. Using the information from the Venn Diagram, write two paragraphs to show how the Galapagos Tortoise and the Marine Iguana are alike and different. Title your work. The first sentence is done for you.

_____

The Galapagos Tortoise and the Marine Iguana are alike and different in many ways.

First they are alike because _____

_____

_____

_____

_____

ISBN: 978-1-897457-03-0

They are different because _____

_____

_____

_____

_____

D. Read the words in each row. Cross out the word which <u>does not</u> belong and, on the line below, give the reason. Write a new word that <u>does</u> belong in the list.

1. turtle   iguana   fish   monkey

   Reason _____

   New Word _____

2. Cuba   Jamaica   Galapagos   Canada

   Reason _____

   New Word _____

3. ocean   park   river   pond

   Reason _____

   New Word _____

4. shoe   crown   wig   helmet

   Reason _____

   New Word _____

Bet You Can't Eat Just One

Popcorn, peanuts, and tortilla chips are just some examples of well-liked snack foods. However, the most popular of all snacks are potato chips. People who enjoy this <u>crispy</u> treat would agree that it just takes one chip to tease the taste buds on the tongue creating a craving for more. This <u>tasty</u> treat was accidentally invented in 1853 in Saratoga Springs, New York.

George Crum was a chef in a restaurant where french fries were a popular menu item. One day a diner complained that the fries were too thick and soggy so he sent his plate back to the kitchen. George Crum, hoping to <u>satisfy</u> the customer, made a thinner <u>batch</u> of french fries. The man was still unhappy. Crum felt insulted and was <u>angry</u> with the customer. He decided to annoy this <u>fussy</u> man. He made paper-thin fries which he cooked in boiling oil. He salted these crispy potato slices and then served them to the man. The customer, <u>surprisingly</u> enough, loved them and potato chips were invented.

News of this creation spread and soon other people began making their own versions of this delicious treat. People everywhere developed a love for potato chips. In 1895, the first potato chip factory was opened and potato chips became available in grocery stores. Today most people would agree that when it comes to eating potato chips, it is <u>difficult</u> to have just one.

ISBN: 978-1-897457-03-0

A. Find the underlined words in the story. Match each word in Column A with its synonym in Column B.

Column A		Column B
1. crispy		A annoyed
2. tasty		B hard
3. satisfy		C crunchy
4. batch		D choosy
5. angry		E delicious
6. fussy		F please
7. surprisingly		G bunch
8. difficult		H amazingly

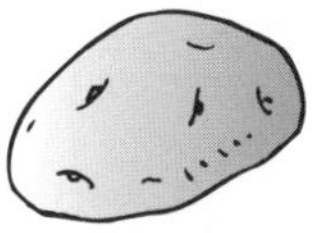

B. You are a reporter for the Saratoga Springs News and have just witnessed the invention of potato chips. Complete the chart below to record important information about this event.

Who was involved?	
What was the event?	
Where was the event taking place?	
When did this event happen?	
How did this happen?	

ISBN: 978-1-897457-03-0

C. **Using the information from the chart, write a news story about this event.**

_____
(Newspaper Name)

_____
(Date)

_____
(Article Title)

_____
(Reporter's Name)

_____

_____

_____

_____

_____
(Caption)

_____

_____

_____

_____

_____

_____

ISBN: 978-1-897457-03-0

D. Look at the following words. Underline the base word. Use the word in a sentence to show its meaning. The first one is done for you.

A **prefix** is attached to the beginning of a base word. It can be used to help find the meanings of new words. The prefix "un" means "not".

1. un<u>happy</u>

    Richard was unhappy because his team lost the game.

2. unimportant

    _____

3. unkind

    _____

4. untie

    _____

5. unfair

    _____

6. unpopular

    _____

7. unsafe

    _____

8. untrue

    _____

ISBN: 978-1-897457-03-0

3 | Barbie Hits the Track

At first glance, Ashley Taws seems to be an ordinary young lady. She loves basketball, softball, volleyball, and snowboarding. She has three dogs and a cat, and a fear of ladybugs. The one thing that does set her apart from other girls her age is that she is a race car driver.

Ashley was born on November 1, 1983 in Toronto, Ontario. She began racing Go Karts at the age of nine but quickly progressed to racing faster karts. Ashley won in many races. At the age of sixteen, Ashley moved from racing Go Karts to car racing. In 2001, she caught the attention of her fans by driving a flashy looking pink and purple car. With her "*Be anything with Barbie at WAL-MART*" car, she finished her year in second place in the overall standings and received a trophy for her sportsmanship. It seemed as if Ashley were on her way to a promising racing career.

Unfortunately, on December 7, 2002 Ashley was seriously hurt in a car accident. She broke her back, had internal injuries, and also damaged her leg. At first, Ashley worried that she would never be able to race again, but with determination she worked hard to regain her strength and movement. Seven months after her accident, Ashley competed in her first race in Toronto. She finished in fourth place. It was a great day for Ashley and for her many supportive fans.

ISBN: 978-1-897457-03-0

A. **Complete the crossword puzzle with words from the reading passage.**

Across

A. advanced
B. normal or usual
C. get back
D. severely

Down

1. likely to succeed
2. inside of something
3. job or occupation
4. showy and stylish
5. prize

B. Ashley Taws is coming to speak to your class about her experiences as a race car driver. Write five questions that you would like to ask her.

1. _____

2. _____

3. _____

4. _____

5. _____

C. To convince people, it is important to understand both sides of an opinion. Read the statement below and complete the chart.

I should be allowed to race Go Karts.

Reasons For	Reasons Against
1. Racing is very exciting.	1. Racing is dangerous.
2. _____	2. _____
3. _____	3. _____
4. _____	4. _____

ISBN: 978-1-897457-03-0

D. **Write a letter to convince your parents to let you play a sport that they do not want you to play.**

Dear Mom and Dad,

    I know that you do not want me to _____

_____ but I think that it is a great idea. I would like to

_____ because

_____

_____

_____

_____

_____

_____

_____

_____

_____

_____

4 Wash Day

A. Read the following story. Use the words in the word bank to fill in the blanks.

towel	shiny	rinsed	lastly
allowed	first	bead	next

Michael stared as his big brother Larry backed his 1. _____ black 1964 Mustang out of the garage. For years Michael had watched as Larry carefully went through the steps of washing and caring for his car. Today was finally the day that Michael was being 2. _____ to help.

3. _____ , Larry instructed Michael to use the hose to wet the car thoroughly from top to bottom. This helped to remove any loose dirt. 4. _____ , Larry filled the bucket with cold water and added a special car soap which made the water sudsy. Michael was instructed to dunk a clean cotton 5. _____ into the soapy water and gently wash the car. Together the brothers washed the roof, hood, and trunk of the car. Michael then 6. _____ these areas with clean water from the hose. Next, they washed the sides and the bumpers of the car. Once again, Larry told Michael to hose off the soapsuds on the car. 7. _____ , it was time to dry the car. Michael and Larry each grabbed a clean dry towel and began wiping the car surface. Again, they started with the roof, hood, and trunk and then moved to the sides of the car. After the last 8. _____ of water was wiped off, both boys stepped back to admire the great work they had done.

ISBN: 978-1-897457-03-0

B. Look at the group of pictures below. Put the pictures in order by writing "first", "next", or "lastly" under the correct picture.

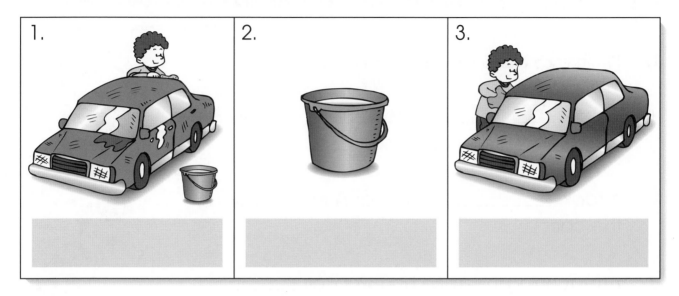

1.

2.

3.

C. Write a paragraph about how to do ONE of the following.

> How to brush your teeth
> How to build a snow fort
> How to care for a pet

Use the words "first", "next", and "lastly" to help put steps in order.

_____

_____

_____

_____

_____

_____

Homonyms are words that sound the same but have different spellings and meanings.

D. Fill in each blank with the correct homonym.

1. Bruce _____ (knew, new) that Michelle would enjoy using the hose.

2. It took _____ (for, four) hours to wash the car.

3. After running the marathon, Rob felt _____ (week, weak).

4. Jennifer wore an old _____ (pair, pear) of sneakers to clean the garage.

5. Can you _____ (hear, here) the thunder in the distance?

E. The wrong homonyms have been used in the following sentences. Rewrite each sentence using the proper homonym.

1. The be buzzed around the flour garden.

_____

2. The wind blue leaves onto the freshly washed car.

_____

3. Michael could sea how special the car was to Larry.

_____

4. There were ate kittens at the pet store.

_____

5. Sandra walked to the store to bye milk.

_____

F. Change one letter in each slide to make the final word. Each slide must be a real word.

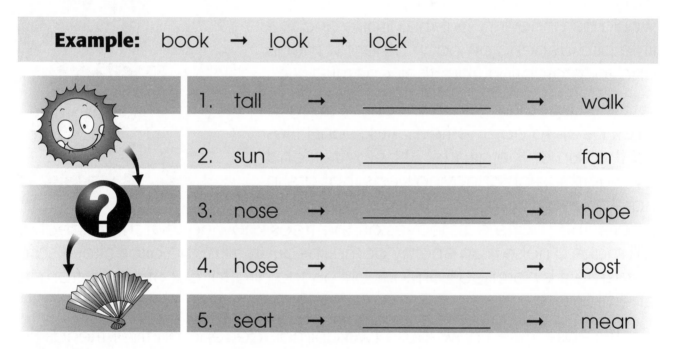

Example: book → <u>l</u>ook → lo<u>c</u>k

1. tall → _____ → walk

2. sun → _____ → fan

3. nose → _____ → hope

4. hose → _____ → post

5. seat → _____ → mean

Make up your own word slides. Challenge a friend to solve them.

1. [   ] ➡ _____ ➡ [   ]

2. [   ] ➡ _____ ➡ [   ]

ISBN: 978-1-897457-03-0

5 Animal Pals

Everyone needs a friend they can depend on. Friends can be great company and will lend a helping hand whenever they can. Just as human beings depend on their friends, animals depend on each other too.

The giraffe is an example of an animal which has developed a special friendship with a small bird called an oxpecker. In Africa, oxpeckers can usually be seen riding on the back or the head of a giraffe. One may think that a passenger of this type would be annoying, but the giraffe and the little bird depend on each other for meals and for protection from their enemies.

The oxpecker gets its meals by using its thick beak to eat the fleas, ticks, and flies off the skin of the giraffe. It helps its friend by munching on annoying pests that are in hard-to-reach places. With its buddy on board, the giraffe eats leaves off the trees knowing that the oxpecker will make a noise if an enemy comes near. In turn, the oxpecker is safe because it is perched comfortably on the giraffe, out of reach from its enemies.

It's easy to see how these two animals depend on their friendship for survival in the wild.

A. **Fill in the blanks to make synonyms for words found in the story.**

> *Synonyms* are words that have the same meaning.

1. **little**   a. s _ _ _ l   b. t _ _ y

2. **depend**   a. r _ _ y   b. n _ e _

ISBN: 978-1-897457-03-0

3.	**munching**	a. _ a t _ _ _	b. c _ _ w _ _ _
4.	**skin**	a. f _ _	b. _ o a _
5.	**friend**	a. c h _ _	b. _ _ l

B. Use information from the story to write an acrostic poem about the giraffe. Don't forget to mention the oxpecker.

ISBN: 978-1-897457-03-0

C. Complete the crossword puzzle by finding opposites.

ACROSS	DOWN
A. The opposite of "stop"	1. The opposite of "best"
B. The opposite of "thick"	2. The opposite of "on"
C. The opposite of "hard"	3. The opposite of "day"
D. The opposite of "small"	4. The opposite of "under"
E. The opposite of "same"	5. The opposite of "top"
F. The opposite of "in"	6. The opposite of "first"
	7. The opposite of "back"
	8. The opposite of "far"

ISBN: 978-1-897457-03-0

Collective Nouns

Collective nouns are words that name a group of things.

Examples: A **flock** of sheep
A **team** of players

D. Match each collective noun with the correct group.

1. A school of ◯

2. A swarm of ◯

3. An army of ◯

4. A herd of ◯

5. A pride of ◯

6. A litter of ◯

A. lions

B. fish

C. cows

D. bees

E. ants

F. puppies

E. The oxpecker spends a lot of time riding on the giraffe. Create a comic strip about these two animals. Use talk balloons to show what they might say to each other.

The Giraffe & The Oxpecker

6 Penelope and Her Plastic Palm Tree

Penelope Patterson appeared to be an ordinary 10-year-old girl. She lived with her mother, father, and her brother Paul on Pine Street in Peterborough, Ontario. She had a pet poodle named Poncho and purple was her favourite colour. Penelope loved to play with her two best friends, Patty and Priscilla.

Penelope had everything she ever wanted except for one thing. She dreamed of having her own plastic palm tree. Her parents refused to buy one for her birthday and Santa did not bring one at Christmas. Penelope decided to take matters into her own hands. She asked her mother to take her to the bank. Penelope withdrew enough money from her account to buy the magnificent plastic palm tree. Penelope's mother then drove to the local department store where Penelope bought the tree. As soon as they arrived home, Penelope placed her tree right in the middle of the front lawn.

Penelope loved her plastic palm tree. Her family tolerated the tree but the neighbours hated it. They felt that the tree made the neighbourhood look terrible. In fact, they disliked it so much that they sent a petition around the community. All the neighbours signed the petition that ordered Penelope to remove the tree from the front yard. Penelope was devastated. What would she do?

Suddenly Penelope had a brilliant idea. She decided to write a speech to convince her neighbours to let the tree stay in the front yard.

ISBN: 978-1-897457-03-0

A. Help Penelope brainstorm ideas for her speech. Fill in the thought bubble with reasons for keeping the tree.

Think Before You Write !

_____

_____

_____

_____

_____

B. Using the information from above, help Penelope complete her speech.

Fellow Neighbours,

    I have gathered you here today for a very important reason. I would like to talk to you about _____

_____

_____

_____

_____

_____

_____

_____

C. The following is a list of "p" words found in the story. Place them in alphabetical order.

Patty   Pine   parents   placed
Penelope   Patterson   Paul   pet
poodle   Poncho   purple   plastic
petition   Priscilla   palm   Peterborough

1. _____

2. _____

3. _____

4. _____

5. _____

6. _____

7. _____

8. _____

9. _____

10. _____

11. _____

12. _____

13. _____

14. _____

15. _____

16. _____

D. Write the contraction for each pair of words.

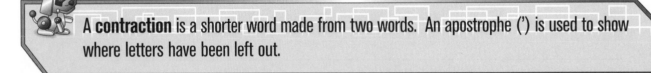

A **contraction** is a shorter word made from two words. An apostrophe (') is used to show where letters have been left out.

1. he is   _____

2. would not   _____

3. they are   _____

4. I will   _____

5. it is   _____

6. I would   _____

ISBN: 978-1-897457-03-0

E. Write the words used to make the contractions.

1. couldn't _____

2. we've _____

3. I'm _____

4. she'll _____

5. that's _____

6. you're _____

F. Using contractions, rewrite what Penelope is saying.

1. I will write a speech about my plastic palm tree.

_____

2. It would not make sense to get rid of such a beautiful tree.

_____

 Alliteration

Alliteration is a consonant sound repeated.

Examples: Penelope played near her plastic palm tree.
Six swans swam slowly in the sun.

G. Write silly sentences using words beginning with the letters provided.

1. **B** _____

2. **W** _____

3. **D** _____

 ISBN: 978-1-897457-03-0

7 | The Night the Lights Went out

It was a hot and <u>humid</u> summer evening. Kevin and his brother Alan were playing catch in the backyard. They decided to go inside to grab a drink and cool off in their air-conditioned house. Kevin opened the refrigerator and took out a <u>pitcher</u> full of lemonade. He poured a glass for himself and a glass for Alan. The boys decided to watch television. Suddenly, something <u>unusual</u> happened. The TV <u>flickered</u> and turned off. Alan tried to use the remote control to turn it back on, but nothing happened. They soon realized that the power was off. What would they do? They couldn't play video games or use the computer. That <u>required</u> electricity. They couldn't play their CDs or listen to the radio. That also required electricity.

Kevin suggested going outside to do some stargazing. Without streetlights, the stars were bright and easy to see. The boys made themselves <u>comfortable</u> in the lawn chairs. Lying on their backs, they saw the Big Dipper, Orion's Belt, and they even saw the planet Mars. It was an incredible sight. Kevin and Alan had never realized how <u>spectacular</u> the night sky could be.

After <u>gazing</u> at the stars for an hour, the boys went into the house. It was very dark except for a few candles that their parents had lit. They wondered what they would do for the <u>remainder</u> of the evening. Mom and Dad had some great ideas. The family spent the night playing cards and board games and telling ghost stories in the candlelight. Kevin and Alan had never <u>imagined</u> that being without electricity could be so much fun.

A.   Match each of the following words from the passage with the proper definition.

1. ⬭ humid   A.   impressive or dramatic to look at

2. ⬭ pitcher   B.   moved with a jerky motion

3. ⬭ unusual   C.   moist or damp

4. ⬭ flickered   D.   formed an idea in the mind

5. ⬭ required   E.   the part of something left over

6. ⬭ comfortable   F.   large jug with one handle

7. ⬭ spectacular   G.   looking for a long time

8. ⬭ gazing   H.   out of the ordinary

9. ⬭ remainder   I.   needed

10. ⬭ imagined   J.   feeling comfort or at ease

B.   Kevin and Alan discovered that there are many fun things to do that do not require electricity. Suggest 4 such activities.

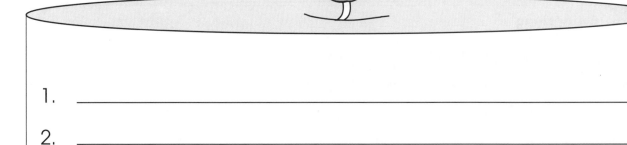

1. _____

2. _____

3. _____

4. _____

ISBN: 978-1-897457-03-0

C. Match the words in Column A with the words in Column B to make compound words. Write the new words on the lines.

Column A

1. down
2. paper
3. candle
4. out
5. every
6. him
7. news
8. fire

Column B

paper
side
place
self
back
stairs
one
light

1. _____
2. _____
3. _____
4. _____
5. _____
6. _____
7. _____
8. _____

Adjectives

An adjective is a word that describes a person, place, or thing.

Examples: The **dark** sky was filled with **bright** stars.

D. Circle the two adjectives in each sentence.

1. The friendly neighbour sat on the comfortable chair.

2. The red planet could be seen in the dark sky.

ISBN: 978-1-897457-03-0

3. The tasty lemonade was made from fresh lemons.

4. The wax candle had an orange flame.

5. The playful puppy caught the rubber ball.

6. My wonderful mother cooked a delicious dinner.

7. The noisy children are running around in the small room.

8. The tired boys rested in the cool shade.

E. Add an adjective to each underlined noun. Write the new sentence.

1. The <u>firefighter</u> sprayed water on the <u>fire</u>.

   _____

   _____

2. The <u>airplane</u> is in the <u>sky</u>.

   _____

   _____

3. A <u>boat</u> took us to the <u>island</u>.

   _____

   _____

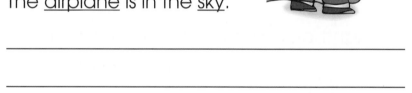

4. The <u>car</u> belongs to the <u>man</u>.

   _____

   _____

5. The <u>children</u> share the <u>cake</u>.

   _____

   _____

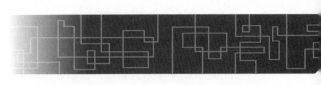

PROGRESS TEST 1

A. Read the following story. Use the words in the word bank to fill in the blanks.

original   tower   traffic
fire   electricity
invented   ancient   guide
candles   brighter

A lighthouse is a tall 1.＿＿＿＿＿＿＿＿ with a very bright light at the top. It is usually located near the coast to 2.＿＿＿＿＿＿＿＿ sailors at night and to warn them of points of danger. The lighthouse acts as a 3.＿＿＿＿＿＿＿＿ sign on the sea.

Lighthouses have been around for a very long time. In fact, the 4.＿＿＿＿＿＿＿＿ Egyptians built the first one, the Pharos of Alexandria, in 280 B.C. It was the height of a 45-storey building. An open 5.＿＿＿＿＿＿＿＿ at the top was used as a source of light.

Later in the history of lighthouses, 6.＿＿＿＿＿＿＿＿ were used to create light until the oil lamp was 7.＿＿＿＿＿＿＿＿ . In the late 1700's, a bowl mirror was put behind the flame of an oil lamp and this created a beam of light. The mirror made the light 8.＿＿＿＿＿＿＿＿ and easier to see from a distance. In 1886, the Statue of Liberty became the first lighthouse to use 9.＿＿＿＿＿＿＿＿ .

Today there are about 1,400 lighthouses in the world. Most of them are automated but a few have been left in their 10.＿＿＿＿＿＿＿＿ state to remind us of their important role in history.

ISBN: 978-1-897457-03-0

B. **Match the following words with the proper definitions.**

1. ⚪ basking	A.	job or occupation
2. ⚪ approximately	B.	moist or damp
3. ⚪ exposed	C.	not exactly
4. ⚪ ordinary	D.	moved with a jerky motion
5. ⚪ career	E.	lying in warmth and sunshine
6. ⚪ humid	F.	uncovered without protection
7. ⚪ flickered	G.	showy and stylish
8. ⚪ flashy	H.	normal or usual

C. **Match each word in Column A with its synonym in Column B.**

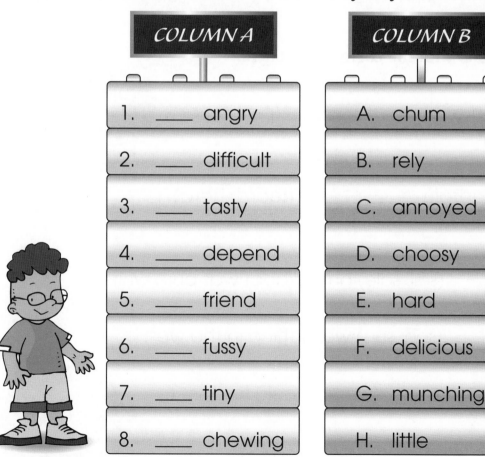

COLUMN A	COLUMN B
1. _____ angry	A. chum
2. _____ difficult	B. rely
3. _____ tasty	C. annoyed
4. _____ depend	D. choosy
5. _____ friend	E. hard
6. _____ fussy	F. delicious
7. _____ tiny	G. munching
8. _____ chewing	H. little

ISBN: 978-1-897457-03-0

D. **Read the words in each row. Cross out the word which does not belong and on the line below, give the reason. Write a new word that does belong in the list.**

1. | dog | elephant | cat | hamster |

   Reason: _____

   New Word: _____

2. | sock | shoe | belt | slipper |

   Reason: _____

   New Word: _____

3. | soccer | swimming | baseball | golf |

   Reason: _____

   New Word: _____

E. **Fill in each blank with the correct homonym.**

1. Olivia picked a juicy _____ (pair, pear) from the tree.

2. The ship's captain _____ (heard, herd) the foghorn blow.

3. The _____ (sail, sale) on the boat was pure white.

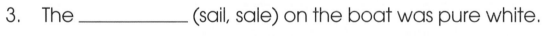

4. The _____ (son, sun) was setting in the west.

5. It took one _____ (weak, week) to drive to Vancouver.

ISBN: 978-1-897457-03-0

F. Change one letter in each slide to make the final word. Each slide should be a real word.

1. son ••••▶ _____ ••••▶ fun

2. nose ••••▶ _____ ••••▶ hope

3. same ••••▶ _____ ••••▶ camp

4. ran ••••▶ _____ ••••▶ cat

5. win ••••▶ _____ ••••▶ pan

G. Match the word in Column A with its opposite in Column B.

Column A	Column B
1. ◯ best	A. thin
2. ◯ hard	B. far
3. ◯ thick	C. worst
4. ◯ front	D. first
5. ◯ last	E. soft
6. ◯ near	F. back

H. Write the contraction for each pair of words.

1. I will _____

2. You are _____

3. that is _____

4. they are _____

5. I am _____

6. could not _____

ISBN: 978-1-897457-03-0

I. **Match the words in Column A with the words in Column B to make compound words.**

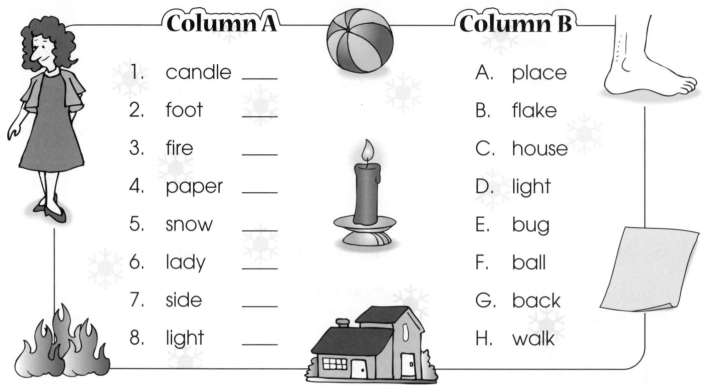

Column A

1. candle ____
2. foot ____
3. fire ____
4. paper ____
5. snow ____
6. lady ____
7. side ____
8. light ____

Column B

A. place
B. flake
C. house
D. light
E. bug
F. ball
G. back
H. walk

J. **Underline the base word in the following words. Use the word in a sentence to show its meaning.**

1. unsafe _____

   _____

2. unlock _____

   _____

3. untie _____

   _____

4. untidy _____

   _____

5. unhappy _____

   _____

ISBN: 978-1-897457-03-0

K. Circle the two adjectives in each sentence.

1. The tall ship sailed toward the bright light.

2. The wise captain was avoiding the rocky shore.

3. The playful dolphins swam in the blue ocean.

4. The tiny canoe swayed in the salty sea.

5. The old lighthouse used wax candles to make a light.

L. Read the following paragraph. Circle the six misspelled words and write the correct words on the lines below.

This summer, Anna and her famaly vacationed in beautiful Nova Scotia. They had a wonderfull time whale whatching, hiking, and kayaking in the sea. Anna's favourite part of the trip was a tour of a reel lighthouse. She learned so many intresting facts. After the tour, Anna sat on the rock and drew a picture of the lighthouse to take home to her freinds.

1. _____   2. _____

3. _____   4. _____

5. _____   6. _____

8 The Three-Toed Sloth

The <u>tropical</u> rainforest is home to a large number of unusual creatures. There are insects, reptiles, <u>amphibians</u>, birds, and mammals. Most of the animals live on the forest floor. Only a few can be found living in the treetops. One of these <u>extraordinary</u> treetop creatures is the sloth.

The sloth is a slow moving mammal that spends most of its life hanging upside down in the <u>canopy</u> of the rainforest. It eats, sleeps, mates, and gives birth while upside down.

A sloth is about the size of a cat. It has a short, flat head, big eyes, a short nose, and tiny ears. It has a <u>stubby</u> tail, long legs, and curved claws which it uses to hang from trees.

Sloths have brown fur but the fur usually has greenish-coloured algae growing on it. The algae act as a <u>camouflage</u> to protect the sloth from its enemies.

The sloth is a <u>herbivore</u>, which means that it only eats plants. It munches on leaves, fruits, and twigs during the night. The sloth can live with very little food. It gets its water from eating juicy leaves and licking dew drops.

People see the sloth as a very <u>lazy</u> creature. This may be because it spends 15 to 18 hours sleeping each day and because it <u>rarely</u> leaves the canopy of the rainforest.

The sloth is <u>definitely</u> an interesting animal that lives a slow-paced life. Perhaps people should be more like the sloth and slow down. What do you think?

ISBN: 978-1-897457-03-0

A. **Use the underlined words in the passage to complete the crossword puzzle.**

ACROSS

A. unwilling to do work
B. not very often
C. certainly or surely
D. tops of trees that form a ceiling
E. very unusual

DOWN

1. animal that eats plants
2. very hot and humid
3. short and thick
4. disguise
5. cold-blooded animals that live first in water, then on land

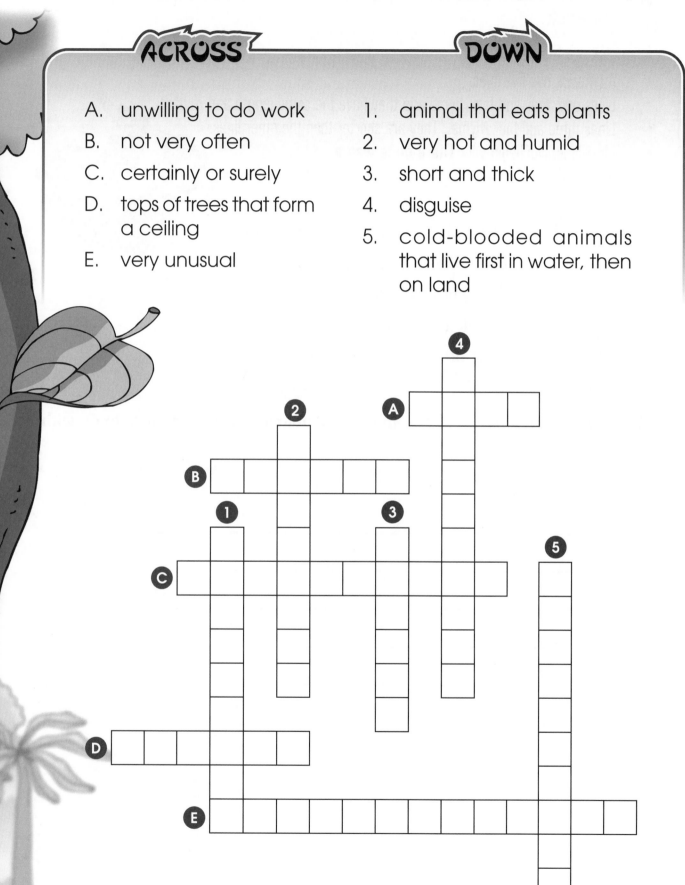

ISBN: 978-1-897457-03-0

Limerick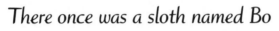

A limerick is a funny poem.

- A limerick has five lines.
- Lines one, two, and five rhyme and they have the same length and rhythm.
- Lines three and four rhyme. They are shorter than the other lines.
- Most limericks begin with **There once was a...**

There once was a sloth named Bo
Who often had no place to go.
Along branches he'd creep,
Upside down he'd sleep.
That sloth he's so very slow.

B. **Write your own limerick about an unusual animal. Draw a picture to go with it.**

Line 1
_____

Line 2
_____

Line 3
_____

Line 4
_____

Line 5

ISBN: 978-1-897457-03-0

C. Match each of the following idioms with its meaning. Write the letters.

An **idiom** is an expression that has a meaning that is not the usual meaning of the words.

1. Don't put the cart before the horse.
2. I have butterflies in my stomach.
3. I was shaking in my boots.
4. I have my hands full.
5. Hold your horses.
6. I'm in hot water.

A. Don't do things in the wrong order.
B. Be patient and wait.
C. I have a lot to do.
D. I'm in trouble.
E. I was afraid.
F. I'm nervous.

1	2	3	4	5	6

D. Read each of the idioms. Draw a picture of what you actually see when you say the phrase.

Who let the cat out of the bag?	I put my foot in my mouth.

ISBN: 978-1-897457-03-0

9 The Dead Sea

Rivers, lakes, seas, and oceans are all bodies of water that cover parts of the earth. Rivers and lakes are usually surrounded by land and are made up of fresh water. Seas and oceans are much larger. They are made up of salt water.

Dead
Sea

The Dead Sea is an interesting body of water because although it is a sea, it is also very similar to a lake.

The countries of Jordan and Israel surround the Dead Sea. The Jordan River flows into the Dead Sea, but there is no place for the water to flow out. The only way for the water to escape from the Dead Sea is through evaporation. Evaporation happens when water is heated by the sun and changes from liquid to vapour. As vapour, water is carried into the air and becomes part of the clouds. As the water evaporates, salt is left behind. As a result, the Dead Sea is very, very salty. In fact, it is the saltiest body of water in the world. Fish and plants cannot survive in this deadly environment, but human beings can safely take pleasure in its unique characteristics.

Thousands of people visit the Dead Sea each year to enjoy its mineral-rich waters. The large amounts of salt make it difficult to swim in the sea so people just sit back and float like a boat on water. The water does the work while the tourists take in the beautiful scenery.

ISBN: 978-1-897457-03-0

A. Match each of the following words from the passage with the proper definition.

1. ____ surrounded

2. ____ escape

3. ____ evaporation

4. ____ liquid

5. ____ environment

6. ____ survive

7. ____ characteristics

8. ____ scenery

A. natural world where people, animals, and plants live

B. manage to stay alive

C. come all around completely

D. features that make somebody or something recognizable

E. natural surroundings

F. get free

G. fluid, not solid

H. a process in which water is changed from liquid to vapour

B. Read the following words. Write the number of syllables.

<u>Number of Syllables</u>

1.	escape	2
2.	environment	____
3.	rivers	____
4.	similar	____
5.	surrounded	____
6.	thousands	____
7.	survive	____
8.	mineral	____

9

Challenge

Find a word in the story that has five syllables.

_____

C. Write the plural form of these words.

Most words are made plural by adding "s".

If a word ends in "y", we change the "y" to "i" and add "es".

For words ending in "s", "ss", "ch", "sh", "x", and "z", add "es" to make plurals.

1. sea _____
2. box _____
3. body _____
4. country _____
5. address _____
6. lunch _____
7. river _____
8. wish _____
9. ocean _____
10. buzz _____

D. Write the singular form of these words.

1. lakes _____
2. guesses _____
3. berries _____
4. peaches _____
5. ladies _____
6. foxes _____
7. tourists _____
8. bushes _____

ISBN: 978-1-897457-03-0

E. Read the question in each box. Write the answer with describing words.

Think about a day when you were at the beach or at a swimming pool. Maybe you were floating in the water or playing in the sand.

Sights

How did the people and things around you look?

_____

_____

_____

_____

Sounds

How did the water and things around you sound?

_____

_____

_____

_____

Touch

How did the water or sand feel?

_____

_____

_____

_____

Feelings

How did you feel on this day?

_____

_____

_____

_____

ISBN: 978-1-897457-03-0

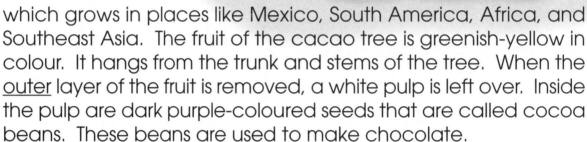

Chocolate

is a favourite "sweet treat" of people all over the world. It comes from the fruit of the cacao tree which grows in places like Mexico, South America, Africa, and Southeast Asia. The fruit of the cacao tree is greenish-yellow in colour. It hangs from the trunk and stems of the tree. When the <u>outer</u> layer of the fruit is removed, a white pulp is left over. Inside the pulp are dark purple-coloured seeds that are called cocoa beans. These beans are used to make chocolate.

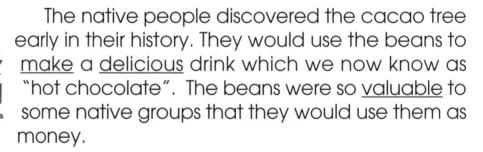

The native people discovered the cacao tree early in their history. They would use the beans to <u>make</u> a <u>delicious</u> drink which we now know as "hot chocolate". The beans were so <u>valuable</u> to some native groups that they would use them as money.

During the age of exploration, chocolate was introduced to the rest of the world. In 1502, Columbus noticed the natives trading in beans for other goods, but he did not understand their worth. In 1519, another Spanish <u>explorer</u> by the name of Cortez learned the <u>secret</u> of the cocoa bean from the Aztecs of Mexico. It became an <u>instant</u> hit when the Queen had her first <u>sip</u> of hot chocolate flavoured with chili peppers.

At first, only the very <u>rich</u> could afford to have chocolate, but soon the French, English, and Dutch began to grow cacao trees in their colonies. In no time at all, people were enjoying chocolate all over Europe. Later, the chili pepper was replaced with sugar. Chocolate began to be used to make chocolate bars and a wide <u>variety</u> of desserts. The rest, as they say, is history!

ISBN: 978-1-897457-03-0

A. Read each sentence. Choose a word from the story that means the same as the underlined word.

1. What <u>type</u> of plants will you put in the garden?

2. Let's <u>create</u> a snowman.

3. The <u>external</u> part of an orange is called the peel.

4. The <u>wealthy</u> man drove an expensive car.

5. The diamond ring was extremely <u>precious</u> to her.

6. The song was an <u>immediate</u> hit on the radio.

7. The children discovered the <u>mystery</u> of the map.

8. The <u>traveller</u> saw many parts of the world.

9. Mom baked a <u>tasty</u> apple pie.

10. I had a small <u>drink</u> of Dad's tea.

B. Make a list of eight chocolate bars. Arrange them in ABC order.

Remember to use a capital letter to name each chocolate.

Chocolate Bars

1.
2.
3.
4.
5.
6.
7.
8.

ISBN: 978-1-897457-03-0

C. Brainstorm three things to fit in each category below. An example is given.

1. **Things Made with Chocolate**

Black forest cake

2. **Special Days When Chocolate is Shared**

Halloween

3. **Things That Taste Great with Chocolate**

Almonds

cool   late

How many words can you make using the letters in the word "chocolate"? Two examples are given.

ISBN: 978-1-897457-03-0

D. You have invented a new chocolate bar. In the space below, design a poster to advertise your new creation.

> *Be sure to give your chocolate bar a catchy name.*

ISBN: 978-1-897457-03-0

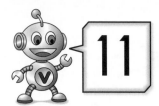

11 Dr. Know-It-All

> Dr. Know-It-All is the advice doctor for Fairy Tale Characters. Below is an example of letters he receives and the advice that he gives.

Dear Dr. Know-It-All,

Today my mother asked me to sell the cow at the market because our family needs the money. When I took it to be sold, a man offered me some magic beans for the cow. He told me that the beans would bring riches for my family. When I came home, my mother was very angry with me. She threw the beans out of the window and sent me to bed without supper. What can I do to make it up to my mother?

Yours truly,

Jack

Dear Jack,

I can understand why your mother was upset with you. She placed her trust in you to make a good and fair trade. You need to apologize to your mother and find a way to earn the money back. If your mother sees that you are trying to make up for letting her down, she will surely find it in her heart to forgive you. Remember, parents want the best for their children.

Good luck,

Dr. Know-It-All

P.S. If you see a tall beanstalk growing outside your window, climb it!

ISBN: 978-1-897457-03-0

A. Imagine that you are Dr. Know-It-All. What advice would you offer Cinderella?

Dear Dr. Know-It-All,

    This weekend, there will be a grand ball at the King's palace. The handsome prince will be choosing a bride. My mean stepmother is not allowing me to go. She is determined to have one of my stepsisters be the next queen. Between you and me, they're quite ugly and don't stand a chance. My stepmother has threatened to lock me up for the evening so that I cannot harm their chances of winning the prince's affection. This is my one chance to be free of this family. How will I ever get to the ball?

Sincerely,
Cinderella

Dear Cinderella,

_____

_____

_____

_____

_____

_____

_____

_____

_____

B. **Something is wrong with the following sentences. Use a word from the word box to correct the sentence.**

| market | broom | freezer | dog | tree |
| axe | bicycle | cat | silk | pie |

1. Jack's <u>cow</u> was barking loudly. _____
2. Jack used a <u>pencil</u> to chop down the beanstalk. _____
3. Cinderella used a <u>shoe</u> to sweep the floor. _____
4. Her dress was made from blue <u>mud</u>. _____
5. The firefighter rescued our <u>giraffe</u> from the tree. _____
6. I went to the <u>library</u> to buy some fruit. _____
7. The robin built a nest in the <u>dishwasher</u>. _____
8. We kept the ice cream in the <u>closet</u>. _____
9. Michael rode his <u>guitar</u> to school. _____
10. Grandma baked a delicious <u>camera</u>. _____

C. **In each row, circle three words that go together. Give a reason for your choices.**

1. apple   cherry   carrot   peach

   Reason _____

2. water   juice   lemonade   popcorn

   Reason _____

3. taco   ice   ice cream   popsicle

   Reason _____

ISBN: 978-1-897457-03-0

4. truck   sled   wagon   bicycle

Reason _____

5. book   letter   magazine   carpet

Reason _____

D. Use the code to solve the following riddles.

1	2	3	4	5	6	7	8	9	10	11	12	13
A	B	C	D	E	F	G	H	I	J	K	L	M

14	15	16	17	18	19	20	21	22	23	24	25	26
N	O	P	Q	R	S	T	U	V	W	X	Y	Z

1. Why was Cinderella such a terrible baseball player?

☐☐☐ ☐☐☐ ☐ ☐☐☐☐☐☐☐
19 8 5   8 1 4   1   16 21 13 16 11 9 14

☐☐☐ ☐ ☐☐☐☐☐
6 15 18   1   3 15 1 3 8

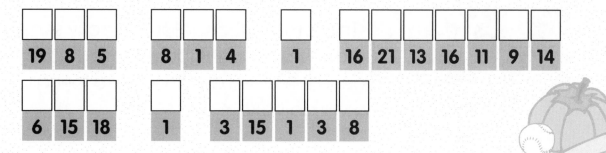

2. What would you get if you crossed the ugly duckling with a cow?

☐☐☐☐ ☐☐☐
13 9 12 11   1 14 4

☐☐☐☐☐☐☐☐
17 21 1 3 11 5 18 19

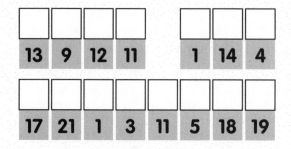

Jim Carrey is a <u>famous</u> Canadian. He has appeared in many films, but is known for his roles in The Mask, Ace Ventura: Pet Detective, Batman Forever, and How the Grinch Stole Christmas.

As a child, Jim enjoyed <u>watching</u> old comedy shows and would imitate and create a variety of characters to <u>entertain</u> his family and <u>friends</u>. He knew he wanted to be a comedian from the moment he stepped on stage for his Grade Two Christmas concert. By the time he reached Grade Seven, Jim was known as the "class clown". His talent was so impressive that his teacher allowed him fifteen minutes at the end of each day to perform for the class.

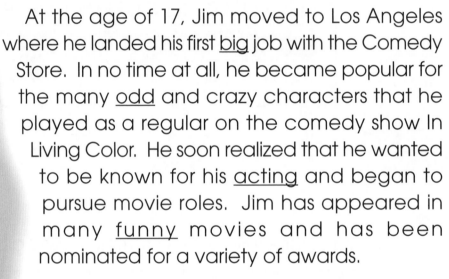

At the age of 17, Jim moved to Los Angeles where he landed his first <u>big</u> job with the Comedy Store. In no time at all, he became popular for the many <u>odd</u> and crazy characters that he played as a regular on the comedy show In Living Color. He soon realized that he wanted to be known for his <u>acting</u> and began to pursue movie roles. Jim has appeared in many <u>funny</u> movies and has been nominated for a variety of awards.

This famous Canadian's wacky sense of humour has brought laughter to audiences around the world and there's no telling what he will do next!

A. Read the story and think about what the underlined words mean. Circle the best answer for each question.

1. What does the word "famous" mean in the story?

   A. funny   B. popular   C. old

2. When someone is watching TV, they are _____ it.

   A. viewing   B. laughing   C. acting

3. To "entertain" means to "_____".

   A. look   B. amuse   C. eat

4. A friend is also a _____ .

   A. pal   B. enemy   C. actor

5. "Big" means "_____".

   A. tiny   B. scary   C. large

6. What does the word "odd" mean in this story?

   A. normal   B. unusual   C. funny

7. When someone is acting in a play, he is _____ .

   A. performing   B. running   C. drawing

8. "Funny" means "_____".

   A. boring   B. laughable   C. sad

B. **Jim Carrey is coming to speak to your class about his life as a comedian and a movie actor. Write five questions that you would like to ask him.**

   1. _____

   2. _____

   3. _____

   4. _____

   5. _____

C. **The following sentences are about people and the jobs they do. Use a word from the word box to complete each sentence.**

dentist	comedian	reporter	stylist
mechanic	veterinarian	pilot	actor

1. A person who fixes cars is called a _____ .

2. A person who takes care of animals is a _____ .

3. A person who writes newspaper articles is called a _____ .

4. A person who performs in movies is an _____ .

5. A person who takes care of your teeth is a _____ .

6. A person who tells jokes is called a _____ .

7. A person who cuts and colours hair is called a _____ .

8. A person who controls an airplane is a _____ .

 Some words help you hear the sound when you say them. This is called **onomatopoeia**.
Example: The **hiss** of the snake frightened the children.

D. **Use each of the following sound words in an interesting sentence.**

1.  bang

_____

2. crash

_____

ISBN: 978-1-897457-03-0

3.  howl

_____

4. splash

_____

E. Comic strip writers use onomatopoeia to help the reader hear sounds. Imagine what you see when you hear the word "splat". Draw a comic to describe this sound.

ISBN: 978-1-897457-03-0

27 Mountain Road
Québec City, Quebec
March 18, 2003

Dear Uncle Marcus and Aunt Rose,

Here we are in beautiful Mount St. Anne, Quebec. I can't believe that I have learned to ski in just one day. I thought it would be much harder and scarier than it was.

First we booked lessons with our instructor and then we were fitted for boots, skis, and poles. It was difficult to walk in them, but with Dad's help, I managed to make it to meet our instructor, Jean-Luc.

Jean-Luc first taught me how to fall down and to stand back up again. We practised stopping by pointing the toes of our skis so that it looked like a slice of pizza. Then we were ready to go on the lift.

It was an amazing view, but I was getting pretty nervous about how I would make it down the hill again. Jean-Luc helped me get off the lift and took me over to the beginner hill. Together we carefully made our way down the hill. I was having so much fun, I didn't even notice when we picked up speed. Before I knew it, we had reached the bottom and I was ready to try it all over again.

Mom and Dad were really impressed to see me ski. They took lots of pictures and clapped for me at the end of the day. I can hardly wait to go back tomorrow. Maybe I'll try a bigger hill.

Love,
Angela

ISBN: 978-1-897457-03-0

A. Think about an exciting place you have visited or an exciting activity you have done. Write a letter to a friend or relative about your experiences. Use Angela's letter as a model.

B. Read the word clues. Complete the crossword puzzle by asking yourself what you do with these things.

Across

A. poles, boots, gloves
B. eraser, paper, pencil
C. soap, water, towel
D. novel, comic, newspaper
E. hammer, nails, wood
F. mop, broom, rag

Down

1. baseball, basketball, dart
2. skirt, sweater, shoes
3. needle, thread, material
4. bathing suit, goggles, earplugs
5. pizza, hot dogs, pasta
6. tea, juice, milk

WORD BOX

| ski | wear | throw | wash | read | drink |
| swim | sew | write | clean | build | eat |

ISBN: 978-1-897457-03-0

"It's" and "Its"

"It's" is a contraction. It is the short form for "it has" or "it is".

Example: **It is** time for dinner.
It's time for dinner.

"Its" means "belonging to it".

Example: The baby played with **its** toy.

C. Circle the correct word in each sentence.

1. The dog was hunting for it's   its bone.

2. It's   Its very cold on the ski hill.

3. It's   Its thrilling to snowboard in Quebec.

4. The bear is looking for it's   its cub.

5. The squirrel collected it's   its acorns.

6. It's   Its been some time since we last met.

Write your own sentence using each word given.

1. it's

_____

2. its

_____

Did you know that I am the Ruler of the Rainforest?

I can roar louder than any beast around.
>   In fact, even the tigers run when they hear my call.

I can run faster than a leopard and pounce on my prey
>   before my footsteps are heard.

I can swing from tree to tree without getting tired.
>   The monkeys eat my dust!

I can change colour better than any chameleon around.
>   I dare you to find me when I don't want to be found.

I can display my fabulous feathers prouder than any peacock.
>   Even the birds of paradise want to know my secret.

I can slither through small spaces and wrap myself around a tree.
>   The boa constrictor is jealous of my skills.

I can snap my jaws at the speed of light,
>   leaving the crocodile with its mouth open.

I am the Ruler of the Rainforest!

 A **tall tale** is an exaggerated story. It has characters doing realistic things but in impossible ways. It includes events that could not happen in real life.

ISBN: 978-1-897457-03-0

A. Match each of the following words from the passage with the proper definition.

1. ruler ⬜   A. extremely good or pleasant

2. roar ⬜   B. jump suddenly

3. beast ⬜   C. slide along easily

4. pounce ⬜   D. somebody who is in charge

5. dare ⬜   E. animal

6. display ⬜   F. make a natural growling noise

7. fabulous ⬜   G. challenge somebody to do something

8. slither ⬜   H. show something to others

B. Think about an event in your life that can be easily exaggerated. Turn this event into a tall tale that you can share with your friends.

As I opened the basement door, a bat the size of a pterodactyl flew over my head.

My Tall Tale

_____

_____

_____

_____

_____

_____

_____

Similes

Similes compare two things using the words "like" and "as".

Examples: The jungle was hot **as** an oven.
The panther's claws were like **razors**.

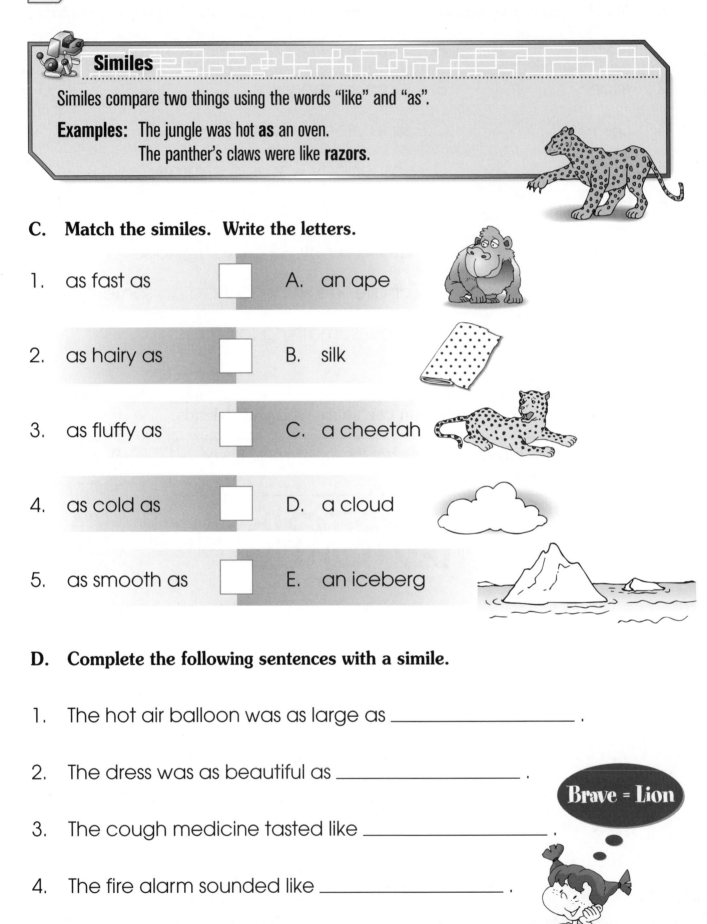

C.   Match the similes.   Write the letters.

1.   as fast as ☐   A.   an ape

2.   as hairy as ☐   B.   silk

3.   as fluffy as ☐   C.   a cheetah

4.   as cold as ☐   D.   a cloud

5.   as smooth as ☐   E.   an iceberg

D.   Complete the following sentences with a simile.

1.   The hot air balloon was as large as _____ .

2.   The dress was as beautiful as _____ .

3.   The cough medicine tasted like _____ .

4.   The fire alarm sounded like _____ .

5.   The necklace sparkled like _____ .

Brave = Lion

ISBN: 978-1-897457-03-0

A **pronoun** is a word that can take the place of a noun. **I**, **you**, **he**, **she**, **it**, **we**, and **they** are subject pronouns.

Examples: <u>Justin</u> is the fastest runner in the class.
He is the fastest runner in the class.

<u>Bob and Mike</u> went to the park.
They went to the park.

E. Circle the pronoun in each sentence.

1. She went shopping for new clothes.

2. We are going for a hike in the forest.

3. It has a beautiful colour.

4. They are going out to see a movie.

5. You look very tired.

F. Rewrite each sentence by using a pronoun for the underlined word(s).

1. <u>Maria and I</u> are going out for dinner.

_____

2. <u>Richard</u> is my brother.

_____

3. <u>The book</u> is very exciting to read.

_____

4. <u>Jennifer</u> is the best speller in the class.

_____

5. <u>Larry and Michael</u> went to watch the football game.

_____

Helen woke up to the smell of bacon and eggs. For a moment she thought she was still in her bed in Toronto but then realized that she was back in Calgary at the Four-Star Ranch, owned by her Aunt Betty and Uncle Steve. Uncle Steve picked her up at the airport the night before. It had become a yearly tradition for Helen to spend her summer vacation helping out on the ranch.

It was 6:15 a.m. and Aunt Betty was preparing breakfast for the family and wranglers who worked on the ranch. Helen jumped out of bed, pulled on her jeans, T-shirt, boots, and cowboy hat. She quickly said good morning to Aunt Betty on her way out the door. Aunt Betty knew exactly where Helen was going.

Helen was at the barn within seconds. She paused in the doorway to take in the smell of fresh hay. Suddenly, a large head popped over the stall door. Dusty, Helen's horse, stood looking at her with his mouth full of hay. He was just as excited to see her as she was to see him. Helen wrapped her arms around the big brown and white horse and gave him a hug. She could hardly wait to put a saddle on Dusty and take him for a long ride around the farm.

Helen offered Dusty an apple. As he crunched down on the delicious treat, Helen thought about all the fun things she would do with Dusty. They would herd cattle, go galloping through the fields, swim in the pond, and at the end of the day, she would groom him to make him soft and shiny. All of a sudden, she heard Aunt Betty sounding the breakfast bell. Helen raced back to the house to eat. Her summer adventure had begun.

ISBN: 978-1-897457-03-0

A. **Place the following "ranch" words in ABC order.**

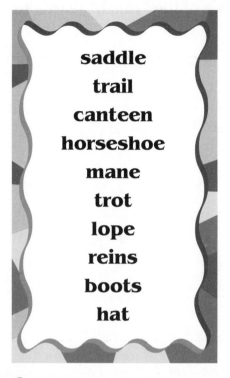

saddle
trail
canteen
horseshoe
mane
trot
lope
reins
boots
hat

1. _____

2. _____

3. _____

4. _____

5. _____

6. _____

7. _____

8. _____

9. _____

10. _____

Postcards are like short letters which are written by people on vacation. The left side is for the message and right side is for the address of the person who will get the postcard.

Here's an example of a postcard that Helen wrote to her friend in Toronto.

June 12, 2003

Howdy Simran!

I am so glad to be back on the ranch. Dusty looks great and I was so excited to see him again. Today we went on a long ride around the farm. We helped Uncle Steve move the cattle from one pasture to another. I am exhausted but looking forward to the weekend. We will be going camping in the mountains. I'll write soon.

Helen

CANADA 48

Simran Singh

12 Cherry Street

Toronto, ON

L8P 1Q4

ISBN: 978-1-897457-03-0

B. **Imagine that you are on a ranch just like Helen. Write a postcard to a friend telling about one of your adventures. Use some of the "ranch" words to help you.**

"There", "their", and "they're" are words that sound the same but have different meanings.

"There" means "in that place".
Example: The book is over **there.**

"Their" means "belonging to them".
Example: **Their** horse is black and white.

"They're" is the short form for "They are".
Example: **They're** going camping this weekend.

C. **Complete each sentence by using "there/their/they're" in the blank.**

1. _____ planning to leave as soon as the horses are saddled.

2. _____ tent was set up in the meadow.

3. Please put the bale of hay over _____ .

4. We will be _____ on Saturday.

5. _____ breakfast is ready.

6. _____ here for the whole summer.

7. Helen is _____ niece.

8. Dusty stopped for a drink right _____ by the creek.

D. Use the animal words below to fill in the blanks.

 kitten    calf   foal   lamb   kid   chick

1. A baby sheep is called a _____ .

2. A cow's baby is called a _____ .

3. A _____ is a baby cat.

4. A hen has a baby _____ .

5. A horse's baby is called a _____ .

6. A _____ is a baby goat.

ISBN: 978-1-897457-03-0

PROGRESS TEST 2

A. **Read the following story. Use the words in the Word Bank to fill in the blanks.**

WORD BANK

jars   stirring   bushels   tomato   tasted

pots   picnic   recipe   sparkling   heat

It was Labour Day weekend, the most important time of the year for the Romano Family. Every year on this weekend, the entire family gathered together to make their supply of 1._____ sauce. They would make enough to last the whole year!

In the backyard, six 2._____ of fresh tomatoes stood waiting to be cleaned, cut, and boiled into a delicious sauce. Mrs. Romano was busy cleaning the huge stainless steel 3._____ in which the tomatoes would be cooked. Mr. Romano was preparing the outdoor stove which would be used to 4._____ the pots. Their two daughters, Rosemary and Pina, had the job of washing the tomatoes.

Once the tomatoes were washed, the family sat down at the 5._____ table and began to cut the tomatoes carefully into chunks. The chunks were placed into the 6._____ pots. When they had filled one, Mr. and Mrs. Romano worked together to lift the pot onto the stove. The pot was slowly heated until the tomatoes started to boil. Mrs. Romano thought about the day her mother taught her the 7._____ . She added the same special ingredients to the tomatoes and stood by the stove 8._____ and watching them turn into a thick sauce.

When the tomato sauce was ready, one important thing had to be done. The sauce had to be 9._____ . Mrs. Romano boiled some pasta and topped it with freshly made sauce. She gave a bowl to each family member and together they sampled the result of their hard work. After one taste, all four of the Romanos smiled because they knew that their tomato sauce was delicious and ready to be put into glass 10._____ .

B.   Match each of the following words with the proper definition.

1. _____ rarely

2. _____ tropical

3. _____ lazy

4. _____ survive

5. _____ environment

6. _____ pounce

7. _____ dare

8. _____ display

A.   show something to others

B.   challenge someone to do something

C.   unwilling to do work

D.   natural world where people, animals, and plants live

E.   manage to stay alive

F.   not very often

G.   very hot and humid

H.   jump suddenly

ISBN: 978-1-897457-03-0

C. **Place the following words in ABC order.**

| tomato | delicious | stove | pasta | boil | recipe |

1. _____

2. _____

3. _____

4. _____

5. _____

6. _____

D. **Match each word in Column A with its synonym in Column B.**

Column A

1. ____ odd

2. ____ watching

3. ____ acting

4. ____ wealthy

5. ____ make

6. ____ type

Column B

A. variety

B. unusual

C. create

D. performing

E. rich

F. viewing

E. **Read each word and record the number of syllables that you hear.**

Syllables

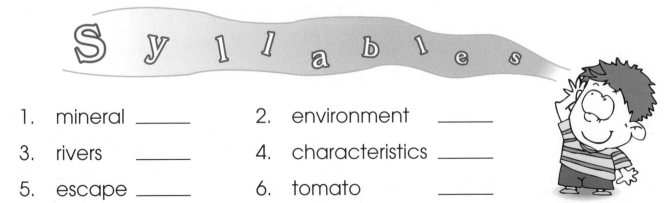

1. mineral _____

2. environment _____

3. rivers _____

4. characteristics _____

5. escape _____

6. tomato _____

ISBN: 978-1-897457-03-0

F. In each row, circle three words that go together. Give a reason for your choices.

1.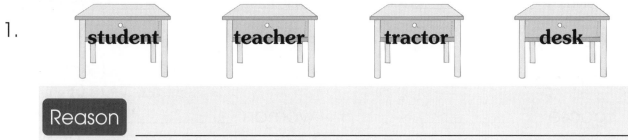

   student   teacher   tractor   desk

   Reason _____

2.

   pizza   taco   hamburger   blocks

   Reason _____

3.

   peas   lemon   carrots   spinach

   Reason _____

G. Correct the following sentences with the given words.

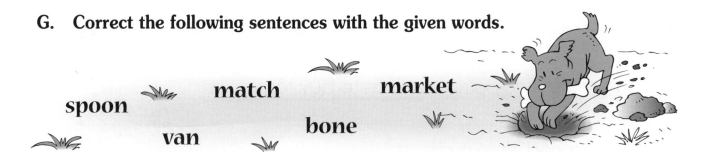

spoon   match   market   van   bone

1. She used a <u>tomato</u> to light the fire. _____

2. Mrs. Romano used a <u>hammer</u> to stir the sauce. _____

3. We went to the <u>library</u> to buy our tomatoes. _____

4. Mom drove the <u>vacuum</u> to the plaza. _____

5. The dog buried its <u>telephone</u> in the backyard. _____

H. Write the plurals for the following words.

 Five mice

1. tourist _____

2. lunch _____

3. country _____

4. fox _____

5. address _____

6. wish _____

7. goose _____

8. woman _____

I. Circle the correct word in each sentence.

1. (It's, Its) very hot in Jamaica.

2. The baby is looking for (it's, its) toy.

3. (Their, They're) going to the airport to pick up Grandma.

4. Please put the jars over (there, their).

5. Rosemary is (there, their) daughter.

J. Replace the underlined words with pronouns. Write them in the boxes.

1. <u>Rosemary</u> is going to the store to buy tomatoes.

2. <u>Sabrina and Josie</u> are best friends.

3. <u>Gary</u> is an excellent artist.

4. <u>Rosemary and I</u> are planning a party for Rob.

5. <u>The toy</u> was under the bed.

K. Complete the following sentences.

1. A young cat is called a _____ .

2. A young horse is called a _____ .

3. A young goat is called a _____ .

4. A young sheep is called a _____ .

L. Match each idiom with its correct meaning.

1. Hold your horses.   _____   A. Be patient and wait.

2. I have butterflies in my   _____   B. Stop acting silly.
    stomach.

3. Quit horsing around.   _____   C. I was afraid.

4. I was shaking in my boots.   _____   D. I'm nervous.

M. Complete the following sentences with the given words.

pilot

veterinarian

comedian

dentist

1. A person who takes care of your teeth is called a _____ .

2. A person who controls an airplane is called a _____ .

3. A person who takes care of animals is called a _____ .

4. A person who tells jokes is called a _____ .

ISBN: 978-1-897457-03-0

ISBN: 978-1-897457-03-0

1 Dolly is trying to catch the ball. Colour her path following the letters in the words "throw and catch".

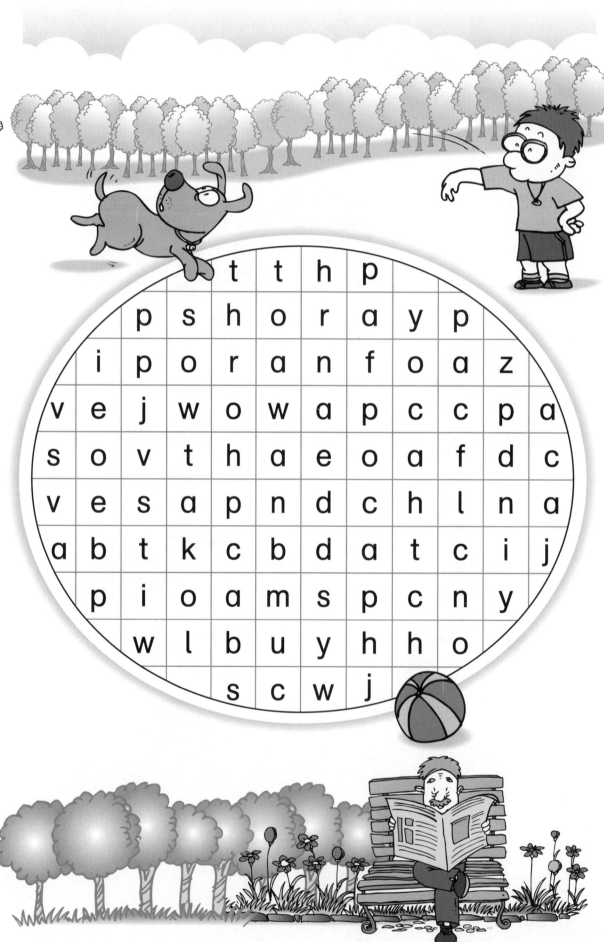

ISBN: 978-1-897457-03-0

2 The animals are making different sounds. Complete what they say.

squeal   bark   trumpet   hoot   squeak
quack   mew   crow   roar

1. I _____ .

2. I _____ .

3. I _____ .

4. I _____ .

5. I _____ .

6. I _____ .

7. I _____ .

8. I _____ .

9. I _____ .

3 Simon the Squirrel phoned home and left a message. Follow and colour the buttons under the ♡ to get his message.

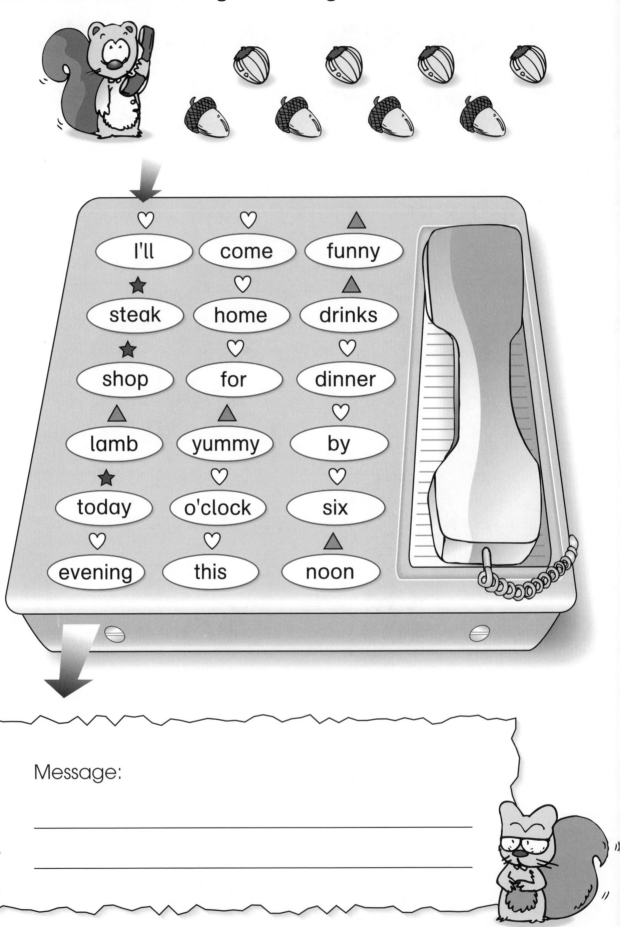

♡	♡	▲
I'll	come	funny
★	♡	▲
steak	home	drinks
★	♡	♡
shop	for	dinner
▲	▲	♡
lamb	yummy	by
★	♡	♡
today	o'clock	six
♡	♡	▲
evening	this	noon

Message:

_____

_____

ISBN: 978-1-897457-03-0

4 It's near Christmas. Help Little Fairy circle the "Christmas" words in the word search.

presents   holly   lights   snow
Rudolph   reindeer   decorations
tinsel   party   Noel   carols   sleigh
angels   Santa Claus

R	u	d	o	l	p	h	l	y	c	p
a	n	e	l	w	a	t	i	s	l	a
n	e	c	p	o	n		g	h	c	r
g	h	o	l	l	y	p	h	m	a	t
e	p	r	e	s	e	n	t	s	r	y
l	N	a		c	l	d	s	n	o	w
s	o	t	i	n	s	e	l	t	l	
r	e	i	n	d	e	e	r	i	s	n
a	l	o	w	k	l	i	t	g	o	d
S	a	n	t	a		C	l	a	u	s
n	d	s	l	e	i	g	h	t	u	s

5 Follow the path that forms "Halloween" words. Colour what you can find.

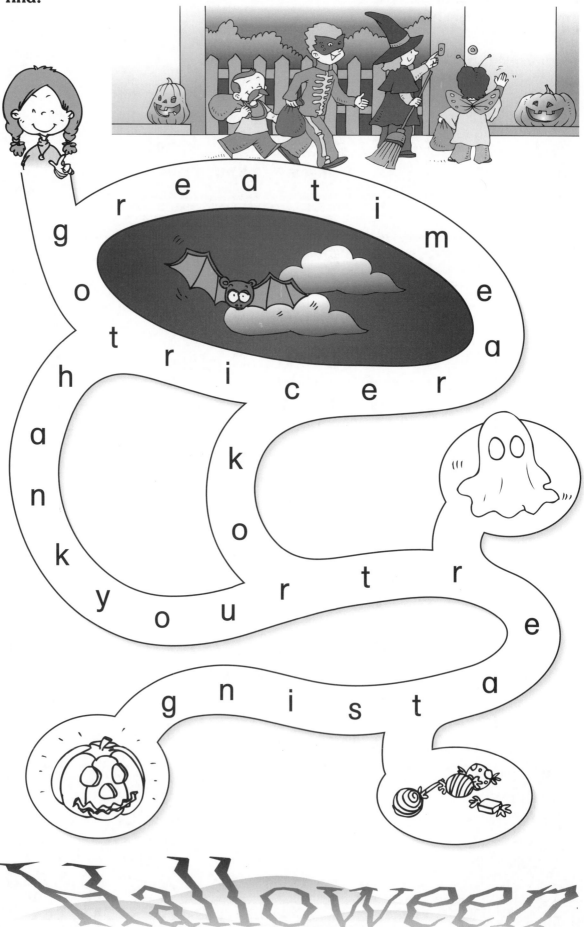

g r e a t i m e a r

g o t r i c e r

h a n k y o u r t r e a

k o

g n i s t a

Halloween

ISBN: 978-1-897457-03-0

6 Look at the pictures. Complete the Fruit Crossword Puzzle.

7 Draw lines to match the three columns of puzzle pieces.

1.   sweet 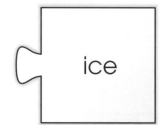 ice

2.   cold  pencil

3.   sharp  lollipop

4. 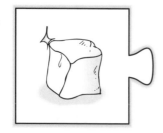  heavy 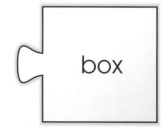 tea

5. 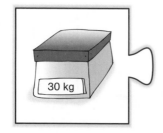  hot box

ISBN: 978-1-897457-03-0

8 Write what the magic carpets say.

1.

how   am   to   I   fly
eager   learn   to

_____

_____

2.

say   fly   "magic"   when
I   you   will   .

_____

_____

3.

but   know   I   fly   can't
I   magic.

_____

_____

ISBN: 978-1-897457-03-0

Circle the "animal" words in the Animal Word Search.

Animal
Word Search

chimpanzee   crocodile
raccoon   cheetah
tiger   skunk   bear
beaver   penguin
giraffe   zebra
kangaroo   lion
caribou

g	o	l	c	v	b	s	k	u	n	k	i
n	c	h	e	e	t	a	h	g	m	h	d
l	f	a	y	r	j	v	c	l	k	c	x
i	k	g	i	r	a	f	f	e	p	h	e
o	a	h	k	a	p	e	n	g	u	i	n
n	n	d	b	c	a	u	c	i	t	m	c
b	g	e	m	c	h	x	o	w	a	p	a
d	a	j	g	o	k	t	e	b	q	a	r
c	r	o	c	o	d	i	l	e	s	n	i
j	o	z	f	n	t	g	m	a	f	z	b
e	o	a	o	d	z	e	b	r	a	e	o
k	b	e	a	v	e	r	h	i	b	e	u

ISBN: 978-1-897457-03-0

10 Circle the present Little Jill gets from Santa Claus by following the three-syllable words.

Christmas

glittering   mistletoe   festival

carol   tree   feast   decorate

present   Noel   gathering   holiday

tinsel   merry   family

JIGSAW

VIDEO GAME

ISBN: 978-1-897457-03-0

Read the clues and complete the crossword puzzle.

Across

1. This unusual pet has a long slender body and feeds on small rodents.
3. If your pet gets lost, you try to ____ it as quickly as possible.
5. You can have lots of ____ with your pets.
6. Pets are like us; they need food and ____ .
8. Many people think that cats can see in the ____ .
9. Dogs can ____ sounds that human beings can't.

Down

1. The long stiff hairs that grow near a cat's mouth
2. Pet food sometimes comes in a ____ (can).
3. This keeps cats warm in winter.
4. Some dogs, such as spaniels, have ____ ears.
5. We should ____ our pets about the same time each day.
7. A pet dog can be a ____ and companion.

ISBN: 978-1-897457-03-0

12 Draw an animal that lives in each home.

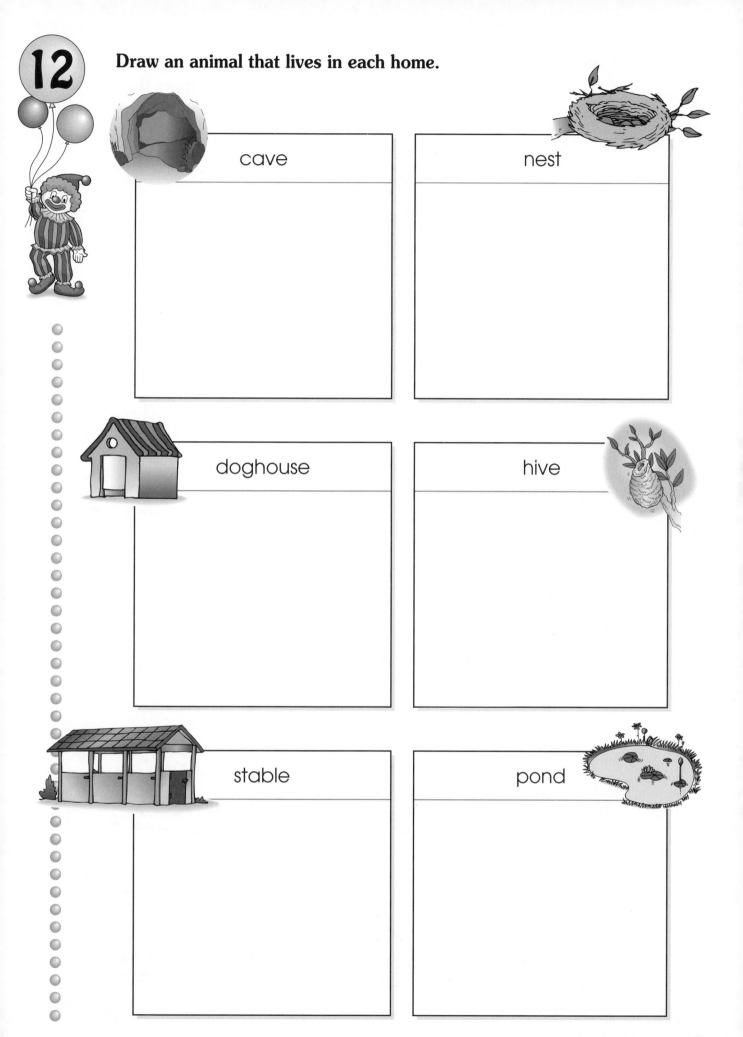

cave

nest

doghouse

hive

stable

pond

ISBN: 978-1-897457-03-0

13

Mother Hen wants to bake a yummy pizza for her family. Follow and colour the slices with toppings that she can put on the dough to help her get to the oven.

pepperoni

clip

ice

ham

chalk

olive

tomato

paper

red pepper

bug

rock

cheese

onion

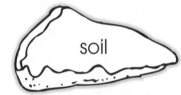
soil

rubber

mushroom

ISBN: 978-1-897457-03-0

Draw lines to match the animal mothers with their babies.

1

duckling

2

owlet

3

lamb

4

puppy

5

kitten

6

chick

7

cub

8

piglet

9

kid

10

calf

ISBN: 978-1-897457-03-0

15 There are many shapes in the Shape Kingdom. Circle the words in the word search.

SHAPES

triangle   trapezoid   pentagon

circle   square   hexagon

octagon   star   rectangle

o	p	e	t	a	m	h	g	n	t	a	c
e	g	t	r	a	p	e	z	o	i	d	k
c	o	l	e	n	p	x	a	c	t	a	g
c	i	r	c	l	e	a	n	t	r	t	b
r	p	e	t	a	s	g	u	a	e	r	o
s	q	u	a	r	e	o	a	g	o	i	r
t	u	i	n	g	e	n	g	o	y	a	j
a	e	t	g	n	o	x	d	n	t	n	e
r	a	z	l	i	a	g	n	i	a	g	u
e	h	p	e	n	t	a	g	o	n	l	m
c	t	d	i	m	u	p	e	d	l	e	q
h	n	a	l	s	f	e	d	p	i	v	t

Complete EnglishSmart • **Grade 3**   ISBN: 978-1-897457-03-0

Matt the Magician is doing magic. Show how he changes a cup to a mug by changing one letter in the word each time.

C	U	P

1. [ ][ ][ ]

2. [ ][ ][ ]

3. [ ][ ][ ]

4. [ ][ ][ ]

6. [ ][ ][ ]

5. [ ][ ][ ]

17

Dr. Wrights can lead you out of the ancient tomb. Follow what he says and colour the path out.

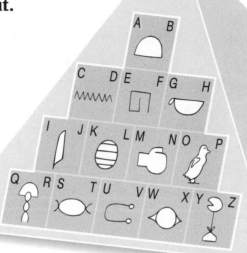

This Egyptian tomb is awesome!

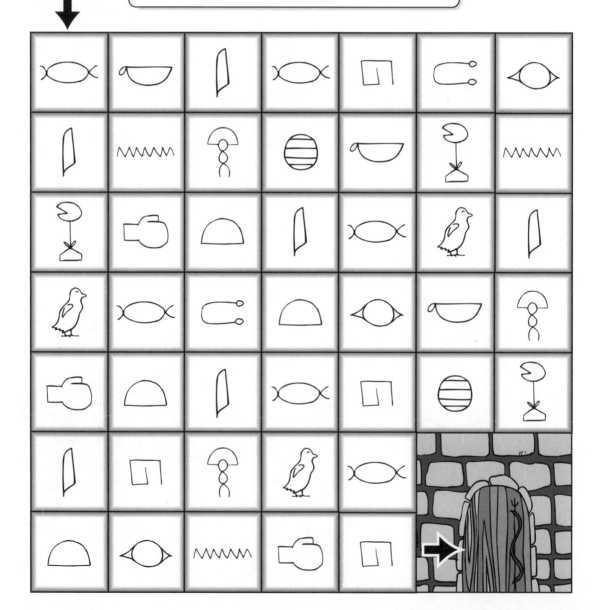

ISBN: 978-1-897457-03-0

18

Look at the pictures.   Write the compound words.

1.   + = [ ]

2.   + = [ ]

3.   +  = [ ]

4.   +  = [ ]

5.   + = [ ]

6.   + = [ ]

7.   + = [ ]

8.   + = [ ]

9.  + = [ ]

ISBN: 978-1-897457-03-0

19 Help Marcia find her lost rabbit by following the route with the words that rhyme with "park".

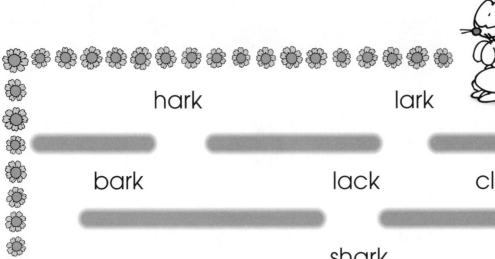

hark   lark

bark   lack   clock

shark

work   dark

dock   make

back   spark

pick   mark   shock

bake   pack

park   pork

ISBN: 978-1-897457-03-0

Read the clues and complete the crossword puzzle on nature.

Across

A. Something white and soft falling from the sky

B. Coloured light seen in the night sky near the North Pole

C. High hill

D. Distant planets twinkling in the night sky

E. Moving air

Down

1. Another name for "shooting star"

2. It warms our Earth.

3. Salt water in which people like to swim

4. Colourful arch formed in the sky

5. The biggest and brightest object in the night sky

6. Large area of water surrounded by land

NATURE

ISBN: 978-1-897457-03-0

1   Nunavut, Canada's Newest Territory

A.
1. The Yukon and the Northwest Territories
2. Iqaluit
3. Because much of Nunavut is above the Arctic Circle
4. About 9 months
5. It stays frozen all year round.
6. Snowmobiles and planes
7. Inuktitut
8. On dogsleds
9. The seal
10. The blubber from whales

B. Common Nouns : manager ; farm ; stickers ; joy ; school ; truck
Proper Nouns : Mt. Albert ; Mrs. Jones ; CN Tower ; Moon River ; Dr. Smith ; Avril Lavigne

C. (Answers will vary.)

D.
1. b
2. c
3. t
4. p
5. i
6. r
7. x
8. j

2   What Makes up Our Universe?

A.
1. B
2. F
3. D
4. C
5. A
6. E

B.
1. (Suggested answer)
An explosion in the universe sent millions of particles out in space. Some of these particles drifted together and formed galaxies.
2. The Milky Way got its name because it looks like a white stream of light.

C.
1. dropped
2. shot
3. fell
4. missed
5. encouraged
6. raised
7. cheered

D. (Suggested answers)
1. gathered
2. swung
3. played
4. helped
5. bounced
6. called

E.
1. pl**a**te ; long
2. d**u**ck ; short
3. p**ie**; long
4. m**ay** ; long
5. st**i**ck ; short
6. t**oe** ; long
7. p**o**p ; short
8. cl**ue** ; long
9. thr**ow** ; long

F.
1. It is a beautiful day today.
2. Yes, it is. Shall we go outside?
3. Let's go to the park.
4. Would you like to come too?
5. Thank you for asking me to join you.
6. I'd love to go to the park. Shall I bring a soccer ball?
7. Look. There's John. Let's ask him to come along.

3   Are We Alone in the Universe?

A.
1. sun
2. water
3. warmth
4. 100
5. extraterrestrial
6. spaceships
7. captured
8. harmed

B. (Individual writing and drawing)

C.
1. Be <u>careful</u> when crossing a <u>busy</u> street, especially on a <u>slippery</u> road.
2. Wear a <u>warm</u> hat and a <u>winter</u> coat.
3. <u>Wild</u> animals belong in their <u>natural</u> habitat.
4. <u>Old</u> Mr. Smith still plays a <u>good</u> round of golf.
5. The <u>dark</u> night frightened the <u>young</u> children.

D.
1. furry
2. icy
3. cold ; white
4. excited ; birthday
5. Happy

E.
1. cut
2. us
3. bit
4. rip
5. tap
6. pin
7. at
8. mad
9. cub
10. fir
11. hid
12. hug

4   Sunflowers

A.
1. C
2. B
3. B
4. B
5. A
6. C
7. A

B.
1. high
2. skilfully
3. directly
4. quickly
5. cleverly
6. swiftly
7. loudly
8. loudly

ISBN: 978-1-897457-03-0

C.

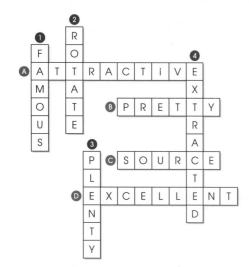

B.   (Individual drawing and writing)

C.   1.   alien's   2.   aliens'
       3.   James's   4.   Jim's
       5.   children's   6.   Julie's
       7.   ladies'   8.   coaches'
       9.   girl's   10.   boys'
      11.   team's   12.   girls'

D.   1.   D   2.   F   3.   G   4.   A
       5.   B   6.   C   7.   H   8.   E

E.   1a. dangerous
       b.   supervised
       c.   enjoyable
       2.   investigate

5 Using Magnets

A.   1.   T   2.   F   3.   T   4.   T
       5.   F   6.   F

B.   1.   holding up signs and magnetic letters
       2.   advertising and displaying names and phone numbers
       3.   used in fishing games, building activities, and board games
       4.   used in machinery
       5.   used in compasses to check direction

C.   1.   I   2.   He ; him
       3.   we ; it   4.   We ; them
       5.   me

D.   1.   We   2.   I
       3.   He   4.   She
       5.   me

E.   1.   crept ; wept ; slept
       2.   hotter ; swatter ; Potter
       3.   gift ; lift ; swift
       4.   snore ; chore ; store
       5.   brow ; now ; plough
       6.   liver ; river ; shiver
       7.   brew ; flew ; glue
       8.   neat ; heat ; sweet

6 Water Safety

A.   (Suggested answers)
       1.   Swim with a buddy.
       2.   Never swim at a beach with no lifeguards.
       3.   Do not run around the pool area.
       4.   Always stay in the shallow end if you are a beginner.
       5.   Check below the water surface in rivers and lakes.
       6.   Wear a life jacket in a boat.

7 Accidental Inventions

A.   (Suggested answer)
      When something is needed, it will be invented.

B.   (Suggested answers)
       1.   He turned an accidental invention into a business.
       2.   It only happened when an ice cream vendor ran out of cups and needed something to serve the ice cream.
       3.   (Answers will vary.)

C.   1.   his   2.   her
       3.   her   4.   our
       5.   its   6.   my
       7.   their   8.   your

D.   1.   His   2.   our
       3.   my   4.   your
       5.   Their   6.   Its

E.   2.   meet   3.   meat
       4.   team   5.   coat
       6.   stay   7.   sail
       8.   bait   9.   stray
      10.   toast   11.   seed

8 The Second Most Popular Drink in the World

A.   1.   A   2.   A
       3.   B   4.   A
       5.   C   6.   A

B.   1.   a   2.   an
       3.   an   4.   a
       5.   an   6.   a
       7.   an   8.   a
       9.   an   10.   an

C. 1. the   2. The
    3. an ; the   4. The
    5. The   6. The
    7. a   8. a

D. 1. bleed   2. clues
    3. chick   4. sleepy
    5. trick   6. crab
    7. brick   8. wash

E. (Suggested answers)
    1. bleach   2. stalk
    3. blast   4. stick
    5. swim   6. sway
    7. store   8. still

9   Fossils – the Link to the Dinosaur

A. Paragraph One: B
   Paragraph Two: A
   Paragraph Three: C
   Paragraph Four: A
   Paragraph Five: B

B. 1. The girls | played volleyball.
    2. His parents | went out.
    3. They | watched television together.
    4. The fast runner | won the race.
    5. The first person in the gym | turned on the lights.

C. (Individual writing)

D. 1. spread   2. stream
    3. scream   4. threw
    5. straw   6. square
    7. street   8. spring

E.

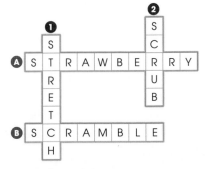

Progress Test 1

A. 1. F   2. T
    3. T   4. T
    5. F   6. F
    7. T   8. T
    9. F   10. T
    11. F   12. F

13. F   14. F
15. T   16. F
17. F   18. T
19. F   20. F
21. T   22. T
23. T   24. T
25. F

B. Noun : morning ; school ; time ; playground ; teams
   Pronoun : It ; they
   Verb : was ; reported ; waited ; ran ; picked ; started
   Adjective : bright ; sunny ; first ; happy ; homework ; furious
   Adverb : again ; anxiously ; quickly

C. 1. (quick) ; quickly   2. merrily ; (merry)
    3. (smooth) ; smoothly   4. (rounded) ; around
    5. (nice) ; nicely   6. creatively ; (creative)
    7. terribly ; (terrible)   8. (secured) ; securely

D. 1. teacher's   2. Jane's
    3. waitress's   4. boys'
    5. Susie's

E. 1. his   2. their
    3. our   4. her

F. 1. a ; The   2. an ; a
    3. the ; a   4. a ; an

G. 1. Winter is our longest season.
    2. Cats and dogs seldom get along. /
      Dogs and cats seldom get along.
    3. The hockey game went into overtime.
    4. How many days are there in a school year? /
      How many school days are there in a year?

H. 1. B   2. D
    3. A   4. C

I. 1. long   2. short
    3. short   4. long
    5. long   6. long
    7. long   8. short
    9. long   10. long

J. (Answers will vary.)

K. 1. slush   2. cream
    3. stream   4. swat
    5. trip   6. sneaky
    7. scrap   8. terrible
    9. throw   10. chalk

10   Are You Superstitious?

A. 1. F   2. T
    3. T   4. T
    5. F   6. F

ISBN: 978-1-897457-03-0

7.   T   8.   T
9.   T
B.   1.   C   2.   A
3.   B
C.   1.   ships ; 1   2.   foxes ; 2
3.   knives ; 4   4.   potatoes ; 5
5.   geese ; 7   6.   boots ; 1
7.   feet ; 7   8.   halves ; 4
9.   enemies ; 3   10.   moose ; 6
D.   1.   basketball   2.   outside
3.   playground   4.   photograph
5.   airport   6.   overflow
7.   homework   8.   nightmare
E.   GRAVEYARD

11   Babies of the Arctic

A.   1.   For two years
2.   Polar bears and killer whales
3.   They form a circle with their tusks facing outward.
4.   For ten days
5.   Because it cannot see, hear, or walk
6.   She smothers the cub in her coat and feeds it warm milk.
7.   They have either fur or fat to protect them against the cold.
B.   (Individual writing)
C.   1.   is   2.   were
3.   come   4.   are
5.   is
D.   1.   arrives   2.   are
3.   is   4.   comes
5.   was
E.   1.   H   2.   J
3.   G   4.   B
5.   C   6.   A
7.   E   8.   D
9.   F   10.   I
F.   1.   surviving
2.   believable
3.   appearance
4.   uninhabited

12   Trick or Treat

A.   1.   B   2.   D
3.   A   4.   E
5.   C

B.   (Suggested answers)
1.   As punishment for playing tricks on the devil
2.   They would go back to their old homes before they died.
3.   When they see a jack-o'-lantern on porches and windows
C.   1.   carried ; will carry
2.   run ; will run
3.   thought ; will think
4.   fight ; fought
5.   tried ; will try
6.   swim ; swam
D.   1.   played
2.   will try
3.   worked
4.   will fly
5.   walks
6.   will take
7.   goes
8.   met
E.   (Individual writing and drawing)

13   Hamburger – the Most Popular American Food

A.   1.   B   2.   A
3.   A   4.   C
5.   C   6.   A
B.   (Individual answer)
C.   My Trip to England

My name is Billy Henderson. I live at 723 Main St. My dad is a doctor and his patients call him Dr. Henderson. This summer we are going on a holiday to England to visit my aunt, Rita. Rita lives near the Thames River. We are going to visit Buckingham Palace while we are there. Our flight is booked on British Airways and we will land at Heathrow Airport. We are leaving on August 11, and returning on September 3. While we are away, our neighbour, Mrs. Watson, will look after our dog, Scamp.

D.   1.   tongue   2.   immigrants
3.   voyage   4.   board
5.   combination
E.   1.   ship   2.   paper
3.   print   4.   board
5.   coat   6.   wood

14 The Origin of Gum Chewing

A.

(Crossword puzzle)

A — CHICLETS
B — BUBBLES
C — SAP
Down: CHEWING, BUBBLER, SMPLE (vertical letters: S E M P L E), BUBBLER
(Letters shown: C H E W I N G; B L I B B E R; S E M P L E)

B.   (Individual writing)
C.   1. she'll   2. he'd
      3. we're   4. you're
      5. weren't   6. who's
      7. didn't   8. hasn't
      9. I'm   10. that's
     11. haven't   12. wouldn't
     13. isn't   14. there's
D.   (Individual writing)
E.   1. been   2. son
      3. would   4. pale
      5. week   6. hare
      7. brake   8. flour
      9. maid   10. wait
     11. hole   12. write

15 The Food Chain

A.   the lettuce ; the slug ; the beetle ; the shrew ;
      the owl
B.   (Suggested answers)
      1. They provide energy for the first link in the food
          chain.
      2. It means to pass energy from one thing to
          another.
      3. It can fly and no animals prey on it.
      4. We would be placed at the top of the food chain.
     5a. lion
      b. polar bear
      c. eagle
C.   1. We won the game.
      2. It rained all day long.
      3. He ate two scoops of ice cream.
      4. Summer holidays are finally here.
      5. The teacher gave the students a test.
      6. The plants soak up water from the soil.

D.   1. B   2. C
      3. D   4. A
E.

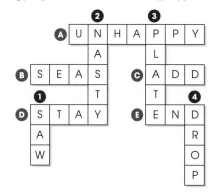

16 The Biggest Pest of the Summer

A.   1. F   2. T
      3. T   4. F
      5. F   6. F
      7. F   8. T
      9. F   10. F
     11. T   12. T
B.   (Individual answers)
C.   1. The happy boy ran quickly.
      2. The howling wind blew furiously.
      3. The talented students sang the songs loudly.
      4. The exciting game was finished early.
      5. John, the tallest boy in the class, was late again.
D.   (Answers will vary.)
E.   1. enemy   2. play
      3. safe   4. hard
      5. calm   6. ruin
      7. empty   8. weak
F.   1. ugly   2. serious
      3. regular   4. dull
      5. wild

17 The Mystery of Migration

A.   1. B   2. A
      3. B   4. C
      5. A   6. B
B.   1. Take your seats before the game begins. ;
          imperative
      2. Which team is winning so far? ; interrogative
      3. The bases are loaded. ; declarative
      4. Wow, what a great catch! ; exclamatory
      5. Is the runner fast enough to steal a base? ;
          interrogative
C.   (Individual writing)

D. (Suggested answers)
1. If you are the first, you will win.
2. He led me all over the place.
3. We tried to convince the teacher to give us less homework.
4. When she lost her cat, she was sad.
5. The students were in trouble for breaking the window.
6. My dad was very angry when he got a flat tire.

E. (Individual writing)
1. Meaning : very special
2. Meaning : tell everything
3. Meaning : going crazy

18 Mary-Kate and Ashley Olsen

A.
1. nine months
2. Trent ; Elizabeth
3. younger
4. "Full House"
5. Michelle Tanner
6. ten dollars
7. "Our First Video"
8. California

B. (Individual writing)

C.

D. (Order may vary.)
happy ; harm ; fine ; new ; pity ; price ; event ; trap ; toss ; sad ; stop ; build

Progress Test 2

A.
1. B   2. C
3. B   4. C
5. B   6. A
7. A   8. B
9. C   10. B

11. B   12. B
13. C   14. C
15. A   16. B
17. A   18. B
19. A   20. A

B.
1. ships   2. potatoes
3. feet   4. knives
5. foxes   6. halves
7. wives   8. deer

C.
1. are   2. were
3. go   4. take
5. are

D.
1. will arrive   2. walked
3. will jump   4. worked

E.
1. Mr. Jones was also known as Dr. Jones when he was at Toronto General Hospital.
2. Linda and Lauren attended Willow Avenue Public School.
3. They took a canoe trip on the Niagara River near Quebec City.
4. We all read the Harry Potter books by J.K. Rowling.

F.
1. she'll   2. we'll
3. didn't   4. haven't
5. wouldn't   6. that's

G.
1. How are you feeling today? ; interrogative
2. Today is Monday. ; declarative
3. Look out! ; exclamatory
4. Sit down and be quiet. ; imperative

H.
1. maid   2. higher
3. brake   4. pair

I.
1. joyous   2. dull
3. smooth   4. proud
5. slow

J.
1. rude   2. empty
3. smooth   4. dry
5. healthy

K. (Order may vary.)
1. fireplace   2. strawberry
3. photograph   4. baseball
5. bathroom   6. forehead
7. handwriting   8. notebook
9. pillowcase   10. grapefruit
11. outside   12. downtown
13. newspaper   14. everybody
15. mailbox

L.
1. E   2. D
3. A   4. B
5. C

1 Nouns

A. Person: cousin ; emperor ; magician
Animal: dinosaur ; beaver ; woodpecker
Place: backyard ; beach ; kitchen
Thing: hat ; stapler ; towel

B. 1. Kelly   2. Benjamin
3. Yahoo   4. pen pal
5. North America   6. winter
7. Australia   8. basketball
9. Raptors   10. Chris Bosh
11. hobbies   12. country

C.

```
                2       3
                G       P
   A  F A M I L I E S
                A       A
   B  C E L L O S       C
        1               H
        M               E
   C  L I V E S  D  S A L M O N
        C                     N
   E  D E E R                 D
           F  P O T A T O E S
```

D. 1. C   2. D   3. E
4. A   5. B
E. 1. is   2. have   3. plans
4. was   5. is

2 Pronouns and Possessives

A. 1. The dolphin – It
2. Mom – She
3. Joe and Calvin – They
4. Dad and I – We
5. Mr. Downey – He

B. 1. us   2. it
3. him   4. them
5. her

C. 1. them   2. She
3. ✔   4. me
5. ✔

D. 1. they   2. them
3. us   4. We
5. He   6. you
7. me   8. I
9. She

E. 1. his   2. my
3. her   4. its
5. your   6. its
7. her   8. our
9. their   10. our
11. their

F. 1. This bracelet is mine.
2. This tree house is ours.
3. That guitar is his.
4. Those pictures are theirs.
5. These shoes are hers.
6. Those rackets are yours.

3 Verbs

A.

```
                2               3       4
                S               B    A  B E T
   1                                    E
   F  E        1  B  F O R G O T         C
   E  A           O              U       D
   A  R        C  D R A N K     G  D  M A D E
   R  E           O              H       M
   E  D                          E  E  W A T C H E D
   D
```

B. 1. laid
2. read
3. found
4. hit
5. studied

C. 1. went   2. helped
3. took   4. played
5. brought   6. was
7. threw   8. jumped
9. caught

D. 1. can   2. should
3. should   4. can
5. should   6. Should
7. can   8. should
9. can   10. can

E. 1. can scare   2. can reach
3. should help   4. should pay
5. can give   6. can take

F. 1. You can open the books now.
2. David can build a house with the blocks.
3. They should not call me names.
4. We should turn left here.

4 Adjectives and Adverbs

A. 1. rectangular   2. nine
3. huge   4. tiny
5. white   6. twelve

B. (Individual drawings)

C. 1. difficult – examination
2. young – woman
3. colourful – umbrella
4. strong – fence
5. stormy – weather
6. exciting – game

D. 1. amazing   2. sour
   3. upset   4. crowded
   5. useful   6. fierce
E. 1. more useful   2. stronger
   3. easy   4. spacious
   5. luckier   6. deep
F. 1. heavier   2. tastier
   3. darker   4. more exciting
G. 1. far   2. extremely
   3. naturally   4. well
   5. quickly   6. sweetly
   7. evenly   8. fast
   9. happily

5   Prepositions

A. 1. on   2. in front of
   3. in   4. over
   5. beside
B. 1. ✔   2. on
   3. in front of   4. ✔
   5. beside   6. ✔
   7. on
C. (Suggested drawing)

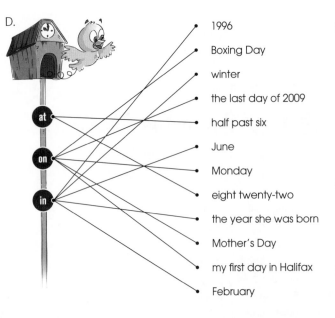

D.

at → winter ; half past six ; eight twenty-two
on → Boxing Day ; Monday ; Mother's Day ; my first day in Halifax
in → 1996 ; the last day of 2009 ; June ; the year she was born ; February

E. 1. on   2. in
   3. on   4. in
   5. on   6. at
   7. in   8. on
   9. at   10. on
   11. at ; at   12. on ; in

6   Conjunctions

A. 1. or   2. but
   3. or   4. and
B. 1. ✔   2. but
   3. but   4. ✔
   5. and
C. 1. A   2. C
   3. E   4. D
   5. B
D. 1. He was sick but he did not see the doctor.
   2. The show was fabulous and we all enjoyed it very much.
   3. Don't forget the password or you can't log on the computer.
   4. We may stay at home tonight or we will go to the cinema.
   5. They love pets and they have four cats.
E. 1. so   2. so
   3. because   4. so
   5. because   6. because
   7. so   8. because
   9. so
F. 1. so ; C   2. because ; A
   3. because ; D   4. so ; B
   5. so ; E
G. (Individual writing)

Progress Test 1

A. (Circle these proper nouns.)
Tim ; Tim ; Tim ; Polly ; Leon ; Jack ; Tim
B. (In any order)
   1. opening ; openings
   2. patch ; patches
   3. member ; members
   4. rumour ; rumours
   5. elf ; elves
   6. fairy ; fairies
   7. cape ; capes
   8. potion ; potions
C. 1. his   2. his
   3. They   4. he
   5. It   6. You
   7. him   8. I
   9. she   10. us
D. 1. Tim still wanted to leave.
   2. He thought the world outside must be very exciting.
   3. His friends tried to persuade him to stay.
   4. They gave him advice on how to make life more interesting.

ISBN: 978-1-897457-03-0

E. 1. can 2. can
3. should 4. should
F. 1. stronger 2. yellow
3. closer 4. special
5. long 6. new
7. really 8. sad
9. upset 10. desperately
G. 1. at 2. on
3. ✔ 4. behind ; on
5. in 6. ✔
7. on ; ✔ 8. ✔
9. ✔
H. 1. Tim finds himself becoming lighter and lighter and he is rising into the air.
2. He lets out a cry because he doesn't know what is going on.
3. His friends hear his cry so they ask him what is happening.
4. Tim can hear the voices of his friends but he can no longer answer them.
5. Is Tim dying or is it the beginning of a new life for him?

7 Parts of a Sentence

A. 1. Ken
2. I
3. We
4. We
5. Billy
6. His hat
7. The party
B. 1. B 2. D
3. A 4. E
5. C
C. 1. The Royal Ontario Museum | attracts a lot of visitors every year.
2. The puppy and its mother | are playing on the lawn.
3. We | brought our own lunch for the farm visit.
4. This campaign | aims at helping the homeless.
5. The heavy rain | caused floods in some areas.
6. Ice hockey | is very popular in Canada.
D. (Individual writing)
E. 1. is 2. goes
3. is 4. eat
5. are 6. fly
7. are 8. want
F. 1. love 2. is
3. like 4. have
5. are 6. goes
7. buys 8. doesn't
9. keeps 10. do
G. 1. are 2. doesn't
3. leaves 4. are
5. belong 6. ✔
7. ✔ 8. Is

8 Types of Sentences

A. 1. . 2. . 3. ?
4. . 5. ? 6. ?
7. . 8. . 9. ?
10. ?
B. 1. The teacher is in her room. / Her teacher is in the room.
2. You can have a piece.
3. Mom told me an interesting story last night.
4. There is a new restaurant around the corner.
C. 1. Who is the catcher? / Who is Jason's brother?
2. Which team is winning?
3. Where is Don?
4. What is your favourite sport?
5. When will we / you play again?
D. 1. ! 2. ✔
3. ✔ 4. !
5. . 6. !
7. ✔ 8. .
9. ! 10. ✔
E. (Individual writing)

9 Tenses

A. 1. is 2. has
3. walks 4. go
5. play 6. teaches
7. learn 8. are
9. works 10. drives
11. are 12. buy
13. enjoys / likes 14. meets
15. like / enjoy 16. knows
B. 1. These roses do not smell sweet.
2. Badminton is not popular in our school.
3. Grace does not have a new skateboard.
4. They do not go to their cottage every summer.
5. There are not many people in the restaurant.
6. I am not hungry.
7. Laura does not want to learn swimming.
C. 1. drank 2. was not
3. went 4. did not wear
5. met
D. 1. We did not rest under the tree.
2. It was not hot.
3. We did not have ice cream.
4. Paul and I were not classmates.
E. 1. will not jump on
2. he will feed
3. it will not rain
4. they will not go to the lake
5. he will come home
6. it will be closed

10 Forming Questions

A. 1. ✔   2. ✔
   3. ✘   4. ✔
   5. ✘

B. 1. Could they finish their project in time?
   2. Does your cat eat beef?
   3. Did the zookeeper tell her the rules?
   4. Do you have a computer in your room?

C. 1. Are   2. Am
   3. Is   4. Were
   5. Is

D. (Individual writing)

E. 1. What   2. Where
   3. Who   4. What
   5. Why   6. How
   7. Where   8. When
   9. Why

F. 1. B   2. A
   3. D   4. F
   5. E   6. C

G. 1. did Ryan stay at home
   2. did you take this picture
   3. can you remove the seat
   4. are you doing / are you reading

11 Contractions and Abbreviations

A. 1. what is – what's
   2. I will – I'll
   3. they are – they're
   4. he has – he's
   5. should not – shouldn't
   6. you have – you've

B. 1. It's
   2. weren't
   3. won't
   4. don't
   5. haven't

C. 1. I'm ; can't
   2. mustn't
   3. She's
   4. We're
   5. doesn't
   6. They've
   7. He's

D. 1. He's been to Italy before.
   2. She'll call us when she arrives.
   3. They couldn't find the restaurant.
   4. We didn't watch the game last night.
   5. I'd rather stay at home.

E. 1. ✔   2.
   3. ✔   4.
   5. ✔

F. 1. Dr. – Doctor
   2. Blvd. – Boulevard
   3. vs. – versus
   4. km – kilometre
   5. Feb. – February
   6. U.K. – United Kingdom
   7. TV – television
   8. a.m. – before noon

G. 1. BC   2. Mar.
   3. Jr.   4. St.
   5. Rd.   6. kg
   7. Mt.

H. 1. Christmas is coming soon.
   2. Her birthday is in August.
   3. The cinema is on Spring Avenue.
   4. We will be free on Friday and Saturday.
   5. New York is on the east coast of the United States.

12 Root Words and Prefixes

A. 1. face   2. clear
   3. able   4. forget
   5. child   6. history

B. 1. sticky ; sticker
   2. silently ; silence
   3. collector ; collection

C. 1. accurate   2. grow
   3. depend   4. flat
   5. build   6. like
   7. contain   8. real

D. 1. A pair of gloves is indispensable in winter here.
   2. Mr. Riggs is a really responsible coach.
   3. I am training my dog to be obedient.
   4. The original ending was not that heartbreaking.
   5. Wow! This pizza pocket is really tasty.
   6. Gary is stacking up the blocks carefully.

E.

F. (Cross out these words.)
   university ; under ; uncle ; unite
   regard ; rear ; result ; reap

ISBN: 978-1-897457-03-0

G. 1. Natasha retold the story in her own way.
2. The stepmother was unfair to Natasha.
3. Natasha found the gate unlocked.
4. Natasha was finally able to reunite with her sister.

13 Compound Words, Synonyms, Antonyms, and Homonyms

A. (Suggested answers)
flowerbed ; housework ; housekeeper ; bookstore ; bookshop ; bookworm ; bookkeeper ; workhouse ; workbook ; workshop ; workhorse ; storehouse ; storeroom ; storekeeper ; lighthouse ; sunflower ; sunlight ; sunroom ; bedroom ; shophouse ; shopkeeper ; horseshoe

B.

```
            ②
            C
        ①   A
        I   L
        M   L
 A C O M P L E T E
        O   D
      B V A R Y ③
        T   G   ④
      C F A M O U S
        N   O   T
      D F A S T   A
                Y
```

C.

u	e	b	l	a	s	t	u	w	i	t	p	n	w	x	b	s
b	o	a	r	n	u	i	x	h	r	u	c	o	l	d	t	w
a	u	o	x	n	o	i	s	y	e	z	r	e	r	g	w	r
s	t	p	g	e	u	v	u	g	q	w	e	h	s	s	e	o
q	s	z	l	v	w	e	x	p	e	n	s	i	v	e	i	n
u	i	m	t	e	q	m	p	d	n	r	q	n	j	s	u	g
w	d	o	u	r	j	p	s	f	t	f	a	r	y	d	s	u
e	e	u	v	m	e	t	n	y	r	f	u	e	r	z	o	d
k	g	i	q	f	r	y	u	s	t	r	o	n	g	h	f	e
c	i	d	i	s	a	p	p	e	a	r	u	u	s	r	t	b

D. 1. sell   2. roll
   3. made   4. hour
   5. suite   6. tail
   7. fair   8. route
   9. jeans

Progress Test 2

A. 1. Tim | is rising into the air.
2. The faint voices of his friends | are fading.
3. All his sensations | are leaving him too.

4. He | is no longer a water droplet.
5. There | seems to be nothing left of him.
6. Everything | comes to an absolute stillness.

B. 1. seems   2. is
   3. He   4. sees
   5. are   6. we
   7. is   8. says
   9. respond

C. 1. Welcome to the Cloud Alliance! ; E
2. What is the Great Jump? ; A
3. It is an event when we jump down to the Earth's surface together. ; T
4. Wow, that sounds exciting! ; E
5. Let's get ready for the Great Jump. ; I
6. Don't hesitate when you jump. ; I

D. 1. Tim is happy to be a member of the Cloud Alliance.
2. He did not want to leave his friends.
3. But he also knew that he could not stay in that cramped place with them.
4. He makes lots of new friends in the Alliance.
5. He will learn a lot from other members of the Alliance.
6. The day for the Great Jump will come soon.

E. 1. What is the name of that large droplet?
2. Is he the leader of the Cloud Alliance?
3. Why is the Great Jump important?
4. Where are we going to land?
5. When will the Great Jump take place?
6. Can I jump with you?

F. 1. It's   2. Mt.
   3. It's   4. m
   5. It's   6. Oct.
   7. What's   8. That's
   9. U.S.   10. Mr.
   11. Ave.   12. Thu.
   13. RCMP   14. They're
   15. there's   16. Let's
   17. what's

G. 1. head   2. loudly
   3. finally   4. some
   5. hard   6. friends
   7. one   8. stay
   9. need   10. nothing
   11. never   12. small
   13. right   14. more
   (Circle these words.)
   reassure ; reunite ; unwise ; replace ; uncertain

1 Creatures of the Galapagos Islands

A.

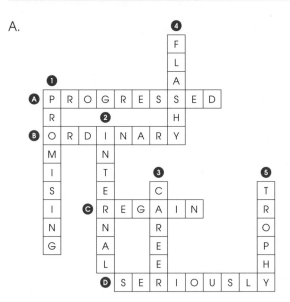

B. (Suggested answers)

Things that are different (Galapagos Tortoise) :

– short feet

– eats prickly pear cactus, fruits, ferns, leaves, and grasses

– over one metre long

Things that are the same :

– live on the Galapagos Islands

– enjoy basking in the sun

– reptile

Things that are different (Marine Iguana) :

– long claws

– eats marine algae and seaweed

– approximately one metre long

C. (Individual writing)

D. (Suggested answers)

1. monkey ; A monkey cannot swim in water. ; alligator
2. Canada ; Canada is not an island. ; New Zealand
3. park ; A park is not a body of water. ; lake
4. shoe ; A shoe is not worn on the head. ; cap

2 Bet You Can't Eat Just One

A. 1. C   2. E
3. F   4. G
5. A   6. D
7. H   8. B

B. (Suggested answers)

George Crum ; Fussy diner

Potato chips were invented.

A restaurant in Saratoga Springs, New York

In 1853

In order to annoy a fussy diner, George Crum boiled potato slices which we know now as potato chips.

C. (Individual writing)

D. (Individual writing of each word in a sentence)

2. un<u>important</u>
3. un<u>kind</u>
4. un<u>tie</u>
5. un<u>fair</u>
6. un<u>popular</u>
7. un<u>safe</u>
8. un<u>true</u>

3 Barbie Hits the Track

A.

B. (Individual writing)

C. (Individual writing)

D. (Individual writing)

4 Wash Day

A. 1. shiny
2. allowed
3. First
4. Next
5. towel
6. rinsed
7. Lastly

8. bead

B. 1. next

   2. first

   3. lastly

C. (Individual writing)

D. 1. knew

   2. four

   3. weak

   4. pair

   5. hear

E. 1. The bee buzzed around the flower garden.

   2. The wind blew leaves onto the freshly washed car.

   3. Michael could see how special the car was to Larry.

   4. There were eight kittens at the pet store.

   5. Sandra walked to the store to buy milk.

F. 1. wall / talk

   2. fun

   3. nope / hose

   4. host / pose

   5. meat

Challenge

   (Individual writing)

5   Animal Pals

A. 1a. small   b. tiny

  2a. rely   b. need

  3a. eating   b. chewing

  4a. fur   b. coat

  5a. chum   b. pal

B. (Individual writing)

C.

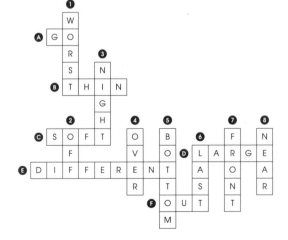

D. 1. B   2. D

   3. E   4. C

5. A   6. F

E. (Individual creation)

6   Penelope and Her Plastic Palm Tree

A. (Individual answers)

B. (Individual writing)

C. 1. palm

   2. parents

   3. Patterson

   4. Patty

   5. Paul

   6. Penelope

   7. pet

   8. Peterborough

   9. petition

  10. Pine

  11. placed

  12. plastic

  13. Poncho

  14. poodle

  15. Priscilla

  16. purple

D. 1. he's

   2. wouldn't

   3. they're

   4. I'll

   5. it's

   6. I'd

E. 1. could not

   2. we have

   3. I am

   4. she will

   5. that is

   6. you are

F. 1. I'll write a speech about my plastic palm tree.

   2. It wouldn't make sense to get rid of such a beautiful tree.

G. (Individual writing)

7   The Night the Lights Went out

A. 1. C   2. F

   3. H   4. B

   5. I   6. J

7. A   8. G

9. E   10. D

B. (Individual writing)

C. 1. downstairs
   2. paperback
   3. candlelight
   4. outside
   5. everyone
   6. himself
   7. newspaper
   8. fireplace

D. 1. friendly ; comfortable
   2. red ; dark
   3. tasty ; fresh
   4. wax ; orange
   5. playful ; rubber
   6. wonderful ; delicious
   7. noisy ; small
   8. tired ; cool

E. (Individual writing)

Progress Test 1

A. 1. tower
   2. guide
   3. traffic
   4. ancient
   5. fire
   6. candles
   7. invented
   8. brighter
   9. electricity
   10. original

B. 1. E   2. C
   3. F   4. H
   5. A   6. B
   7. D   8. G

C. 1. C   2. E
   3. F   4. B
   5. A   6. D
   7. H   8. G

D. (Suggested answers)
   1. elephant ; An elephant is not a pet. ; rabbit
   2. belt ; A belt is not worn on the feet. ; boot

3. swimming ; Swimming does not involve a ball. ; football

E. 1. pear
   2. heard
   3. sail
   4. sun
   5. week

F. 1. sun
   2. nope / hose
   3. came
   4. rat / can
   5. pin

G. 1. C   2. E
   3. A   4. F
   5. D   6. B

H. 1. I'll
   2. You're
   3. that's
   4. they're
   5. I'm
   6. couldn't

I. 1. D   2. F
   3. A   4. G
   5. B   6. E
   7. H   8. C

J. (Individual writing of each word in a sentence)
   1. un<u>safe</u>
   2. un<u>lock</u>
   3. un<u>tie</u>
   4. un<u>tidy</u>
   5. un<u>happy</u>

K. 1. tall ; bright
   2. wise ; rocky
   3. playful ; blue
   4. tiny ; salty
   5. old ; wax

L. 1. famaly → family
   2. wonderfull → wonderful
   3. whatching → watching
   4. reel → real
   5. intresting → interesting
   6. freinds → friends

8 The Three-Toed Sloth

A.

```
                        4
                        C
        2         A L A Z Y
        T         M
  B  R A R E L Y   O
     1     O     3 U
     H     P     S F
  C D E F I N I T E L Y    5
     R     C     U A       A
     B     A     B G       M
     I     L     B E       P
     V     Y     Y         H
  D C A N O P Y            I
     R                     B
     E  E X T R A O R D I N A R Y
                           N
                           S
```

B. (Individual writing)

C. 1. A   2. F
   3. E   4. C
   5. B   6. D

D. (Individual drawings)

9 The Dead Sea

A. 1. C   2. F
   3. H   4. G
   5. A   6. B
   7. D   8. E

B. 2. 4   3. 2
   4. 3   5. 3
   6. 2   7. 2
   8. 3

Challenge
   evaporation / characteristics

C. 1. seas
   2. boxes
   3. bodies
   4. countries
   5. addresses
   6. lunches
   7. rivers
   8. wishes
   9. oceans
   10. buzzes

D. 1. lake
   2. guess
   3. berry
   4. peach
   5. lady
   6. fox
   7. tourist
   8. bush

E. (Individual answers)

10 The Story of Chocolate

A. 1. variety
   2. make
   3. outer
   4. rich
   5. valuable
   6. instant
   7. secret
   8. explorer
   9. delicious
   10. sip

B. (Individual answers)

C. (Individual answers)

Challenge
   (Suggested answers)
    cola ; hot ; hole ; coal ; lot ; cole ; cot ; eat ; ate ; tea ;
    hoe ; ale ; let ; tale ; hale ; hoot ; loot ; tool ; hoe

D. (Individual design)

11 Dr. Know-It-All

A. (Individual writing)

B. 1. dog
   2. an axe
   3. broom
   4. silk
   5. cat
   6. market
   7. tree
   8. freezer
   9. bicycle
   10. pie

C. (Suggested answers)

1. apple ; cherry ; peach
   They are all fruits.
2. water ; juice ; lemonade
   They are all things you can drink.
3. ice ; ice cream ; popsicle
   They are all things that are cold.
4. truck ; wagon ; bicycle
   They are all things with wheels.
5. book ; letter ; magazine
   They are all things that can be read.

D. 1. SHE HAD A PUMPKIN FOR A COACH
   2. MILK AND QUACKERS

12 Jim Carrey

A. 1. B   2. A
   3. B   4. A
   5. C   6. B
   7. A   8. B

B. (Individual writing)

C. 1. mechanic
   2. veterinarian
   3. reporter
   4. actor
   5. dentist
   6. comedian
   7. stylist
   8. pilot

D. (Individual writing)

E. (Individual drawing)

13 A Friendly Letter

A. (Individual writing)

B.

C. 1. its
   2. It's
   3. It's
   4. its
   5. its
   6. It's

Challenge
   (Individual writing)

14 A Tall Tale

A. 1. D   2. F
   3. E   4. B
   5. G   6. H
   7. A   8. C

B. (Individual writing)

C. 1. C   2. A
   3. D   4. E
   5. B

D. (Individual writing)

E. 1. She
   2. We
   3. It
   4. They
   5. You

F. 1. We are going out for dinner.
   2. He is my brother.
   3. It is very exciting to read.
   4. She is the best speller in the class.
   5. They went to watch the football game.

15 The Four-Star Ranch

A. 1. boots
   2. canteen
   3. hat
   4. horseshoe
   5. lope
   6. mane
   7. reins
   8. saddle
   9. trail
   10. trot

B. (Individual writing)

C. 1. They're

ISBN: 978-1-897457-03-0

2. Their
3. there
4. there
5. Their
6. They're
7. their
8. there

D. 1. lamb
2. calf
3. kitten
4. chick
5. foal
6. kid

Progress Test 2

A. 1. tomato
2. bushels
3. pots
4. heat
5. picnic
6. sparkling
7. recipe
8. stirring
9. tasted
10. jars

B. 1. F   2. G
3. C   4. E
5. D   6. H
7. B   8. A

C. 1. boil
2. delicious
3. pasta
4. recipe
5. stove
6. tomato

D. 1. B   2. F
3. D   4. E
5. C   6. A

E. 1. 3   2. 4
3. 2   4. 5
5. 2   6. 3

F. (Suggested answers)
1. student ; teacher ; desk

They are things you find in a school.
2. pizza ; taco ; hamburger
They are things that you eat.
3. peas ; carrots ; spinach
They are all vegetables.

G. 1. match
2. spoon
3. market
4. van
5. bone

H. 1. tourists
2. lunches
3. countries
4. foxes
5. addresses
6. wishes
7. geese
8. women

I. 1. It's
2. its
3. They're
4. there
5. their

J. 1. She
2. They
3. He
4. We
5. It

K. 1. kitten
2. foal
3. kid
4. lamb

L. 1. A   2. D
3. B   4. C

M. 1. dentist
2. pilot
3. veterinarian
4. comedian

1.

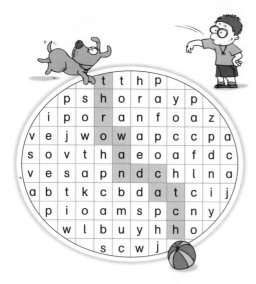

2. 1. bark
   3. quack
   5. squeak
   7. squeal
   9. mew

   2. trumpet
   4. roar
   6. crow
   8. hoot

3.

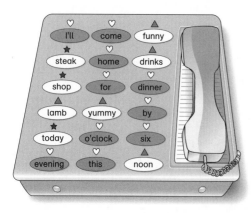

Message:
I'll come home for dinner by six o'clock this evening.

4.

R	u	d	o	l	p	h	l	y	c	p
a	n	e	l	w	a	t	i	s	l	a
n	e	c	p	o	n		g	h	c	r
g	h	o	l	l	y	p	h	m	a	t
e	p	r	e	s	e	n	t	s	r	y
I	N	a		c	l	d	s	n	o	w
s	o	t	i	n	s	e	l	t	l	
r	e	i	n	d	e	e	r	i	s	n
a	l	o	w	k	l	i	t	g	o	d
S	a	n	t	a		C	l	a	u	s
n	d	s	l	e	i	g	h	t	u	s

5.

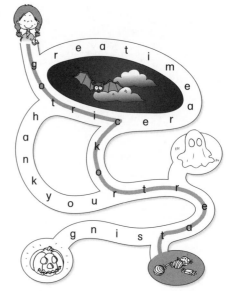

6.

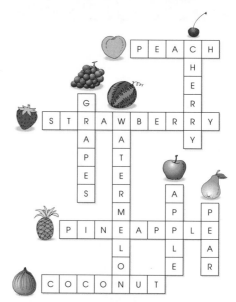

7.

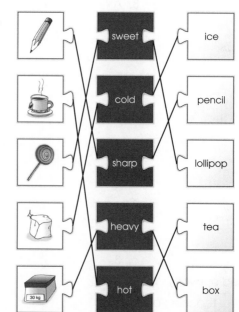

8. 1. I am eager to learn how to fly.
   2. I will fly when you say "magic".
   3. I know magic but I can't fly. /
   I can't fly but I know magic.

9.

g	o	l	c	v	b	s	k	u	n	k	i
n	c	h	e	e	t	a	h	g	m	h	d
l	f	a	y	r	j	v	c	l	k	c	x
i	k	g	i	r	a	f	f	e	p	h	e
o	a	h	k	a	p	e	n	g	u	i	n
n	n	d	b	c	a	u	c	i	t	m	c
b	g	e	m	c	h	x	o	w	a	p	a
d	a	j	g	o	k	t	e	b	q	a	r
c	r	o	c	o	d	i	l	e	s	n	i
j	o	z	f	n	t	g	m	a	f	z	b
e	o	a	o	d	z	e	b	r	a	e	o
k	b	e	a	v	e	r	h	i	b	e	u

12. (Individual drawings)

13.

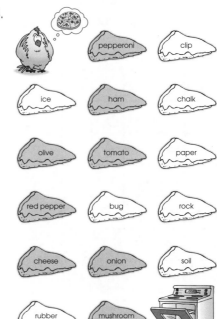

pepperoni · clip · ice · ham · chalk · olive · tomato · paper · red pepper · bug · rock · cheese · onion · soil · rubber · mushroom

10.

Christmas · glittering · mistletoe · festival · carol · tree · feast · decorate · present · Noel · gathering · holiday · tinsel · merry · family

14.

duckling · owlet · lamb · puppy · kitten · chick · cub · piglet · kid · calf

11.

¹W	E	A	S	E	L		²T		
H						³F	I	N	D
I			⁴F		⁵F	U	N		
⁶S	H	E	L	T	E	R			
K			O		E		⁷F		
E			P		⁸D	A	R	K	
R			P				I		
S			Y			⁹H	E	A	R
							N		
							D		

15.

o	p	e	t	a	m	h	g	n	t	a	c
e	g	t	r	a	p	e	z	o	i	d	k
c	o	l	e	n	p	x	a	c	t	a	g
c	i	r	c	l	e	a	n	t	r	t	b
r	p	e	t	a	s	g	u	a	e	r	o
s	q	u	a	r	e	o	a	g	o	i	r
t	u	i	n	g	e	n	g	o	y	a	j
a	e	t	g	n	o	x	d	n	t	n	e
r	a	z	l	i	a	g	n	i	a	g	u
e	h	p	e	n	t	a	g	o	n	l	m
c	t	d	i	m	u	p	e	d	l	e	q
h	n	a	l	s	f	e	d	p	i	v	t

16. 1. CUB   2. SUB
    3. SUN   4. BUN
    5. BUG   6. MUG

20.

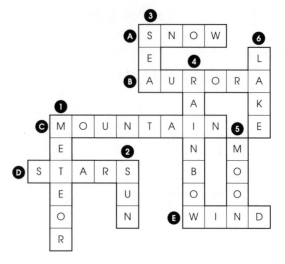

17.

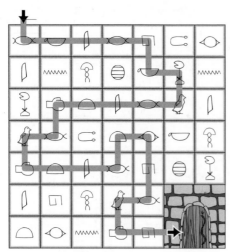

18. 1. honeycomb
    2. starfish
    3. keyboard
    4. headquarters
    5. firewood
    6. bookworm
    7. nutshell
    8. cupcake
    9. rainbow

19.

ISBN: 978-1-897457-03-0